Departed Days

Douglas Tregenza

TRURAN

First published in 1984
by Dyllansow Truran
Trewolsta, Trewirgie,
Redruth, Cornwall.

©*Douglas Tregenza* 1984   B.1898

*Printed by Penwell Ltd.,
Parkwood, Callington,
Cornwall, Britain.*

ISBN 0 907566 98 7

To my wife, Anne

Foreword

I feel that there may be errors in my book — errors of fact, of assumption. I have tried to be as accurate as possible, but where I have spoken of things I have not myself experienced it has not been possible always to make a thorough check, especially when I have had to consider differing accounts from those who have been kind enough to help me.

In any case, I hope that any inaccuracies which have crept into my book will not mar the story I have tried to tell of happenings long ago.

Douglas Tregenza.

Contents

1. Paul. The Pleasant Inn	1
2. The Church. Change and Decay	7
3. Down the Lane to Mousehole	15
4. The Millpool. Feeling for Granite	26
5. The Early Luggers. A Literary Contest	31
6. Hevva!	35
7. The Mackerel-Drivers. Fitting Out	41
8. The Mackerel Fishery	47
9. The Herring Fishery. Life at the Barbican	50
10. Disasters at Sea	59
11. Dangers in the Harbour	64
12. Magic Nights at Sea	69
13. What became of the Luggers?	71
14. The Galas	73
15. The Chapel and Revival Services	76
16. The Ship Inn	80
17. The Shops and Susan Mary's	84
18. The Cave and the Meadows. The Guides	87
19. The Shoemakers	92
20. The Barbers' Shops	96
21. Books	99
22. Model Luggers. Regattas. Magic Coves	102
23. The Salvation Army	108
24. Rescues at Sea, and Tragedy	112
25. Memorials and Poem: "Toll for the Brave", in honour of the crew of the lifeboat "Solomon Browne"	115

List of Illustrations

1. Steps and Gate into Churchyard at Paul, by Stanhope Forbes — 11
2. Penolva, by Stanhope Forbes — 17
3. St. Clement's Island — 22
4. Stone Pillar on Island — 24
5. "The Millpool", by Jack Pender — 28
6. "Tucking a School of Pilchards", by Percy Craft — 36
7. The Luggers. Picture by Stanhope Forbes — 46
8. "Running for Harbour", by Jack Pender — 60
9. "I think I'll be a sailor". Picture by Walter Langley — 103
10. The Sailing Barge, "Baltic", ashore on the Island — 113
11. The crew of the "Lady White" — 113

Grateful thanks for generous help to:

Ned Downing
Harry Drew
Johnny Drew
Philip Hutchings
Teare Kelynack
Raymond Kneebone
Owen Ladner
Urwin Mc.Clary
Jack Pender (senior)
Jack Pender (junior)
Sid Pender
Sylvia Johns
Wilfrid Pender
Arthur Richards
David Sleeman
Vaughan Tregenza
Jack Wallis
Jack Waters
Sid Waters
Reg Watkins
Jack Worth and others

Thanks also, for permission to use their pictures to:

Barclay's Bank, Penzance: Painting of Luggers.
Penzance Town Council "Tucking a School of Pilchards", and Picture of Penolva.
Mrs. Beaumont Varco: "I think I'll be a sailor".
Jack Pender: "The Millpool" and "Running for Harbour".
David Messum Gallery at Beaconsfield: Steps and Gateway into Churchyard at Paul.

To Basil Hall, for encouragement.

And, finally, thanks to my daughter, Mary, for her enthusiasm and accurate typing of my manuscript.

I
Paul. The Pleasant Inn.

I am old. In the pleasant Inn at Paul where I have for some time now enjoyed the companionship of many clever and interesting friends, I have been able at times to tell something of the past as it concerned the villages of Paul and Mousehole; to answer questions put to me, perchance by the lady behind the bar, perchance by some visitor, as to the life of those times.

I believe that I am now at least the doyen of the small company gathered there, many of my older friends having passed away.

It is understandable if at times I go a little beyond merely answering the questions put to me, and in my enthusiasm attach myself too closely to the days long gone by, the days of my happy boyhood in Mousehole and Paul.

Not always do I mingle with my companions. Indeed, as the landlady knows, I like to sit apart, especially at night, and in the dim lighting enter a sort of dream, a slumberous pleasure that is enhanced by the slow hum of conversation from which I have detached myself for a while. Intruding pleasurably for me sometimes in the past into that dream world would come, latish, to sit beside me, David, the London boy who tired of the great city and came as far west from it as he could to a slower tempo of life in this village that he came to love. I was overawed at times by his intelligence. His knowledge of books was extensive indeed, and he could speak of things that were beyond my comprehension. I have referred to him as a boy, for even close on middle age he retained a remarkably young appearance. He was small in stature, rather frail, bravely conscious of a dangerous heart condition which finally and unexpectedly took him away. Now that he is gone I am sad, but glad that he found something, at least, in my company go give him pleasure.

At rare moments, of an evening, a lady with a compelling presence would enter and sit beside me — a fragile, sylph-like creature with the face of a flower, delightful to talk to, glowing, enthusiastic for a cause, but elusive, unpredictable. She could not be captured, only for a fleeting moment. She was David's first love. So David told me.

I feel at times how fortunate I am to have fallen into the companionship of such a varied group of interesting people. There was Paul, potter and astrologer, enquirer into all sorts of mysteries, especially of the subconscious; agog with the possibilities of space; a man old, but remarkably young, with the fresh enthusiasms of a boy.

There was a rather sad man who sat at the bar, pleasant to talk to, intelligent, polite. He could tell, I am sure, of the time he was Squadron Leader, distinguished in the War, but he never did. I had the impression, as I took the drink he offered, that the grim past, the terrors of the prison camp, were with him still, latent, sapping at his initiative, destroying his peace. He leant over the bar, avid for companionship, and I remember with great pleasure the conversations we had.

A lady artist who reminded me of Italy and the south liked to talk to me, not usually of art, but of poetry. We could never quite agree, because, whilst she seemed to favour the obscurities of modern verse and lack of the old rhyme patterns, I would insist upon the need for clarity, and, above all, melody, the music of words. When she asked me what I thought of many modern poems, even of the much vaunted "Waste Land", I had to say that I found them hopelessly obscure, devoid of musical quality, uninspiring, dull, depressing in the extreme. In daring to oppose her I had in mind Molière's great play, *"Le Misanthrope"*, in which the character Alceste is placed in the difficult and unenviable position of being asked his opinion of a "sonnet" presented to him by the courtier Oronte — a sonnet written in the obscure and affected language of the Court poets of that time. Alceste is reluctant to give a judgement, and cleverly delays, but finally has to tell his friend bluntly that the sonnet presented to him is full of conceits and affectation, devoid of merit. As a model worthy of being followed, Alceste presents to him then a little poem of love, written in delightfully clear and natural language, and all suggestive of a song. I have never forgotten this classic instance of a claim for clarity and music in verse.

In my mind also as I talked to the lady were some lines of the French poet Verlaine. In his *"Art Poétique"*, he formulated certain rules which were to influence a whole succession of French poets, including the school known as *"Les Symbolistes"* — rules which would certainly be acceptable, many of them, to the young poets of today. I do not wish to criticise what is a lovely poem, in spite of, among other things, a preference the poet had for *"le vers impair"* — a line consisting of an odd number of syllables, which can certainly be very awkward generally, but which in this particular poem sounds happy enough, being in the hands of an expert.

What is striking in this poem is that Verlaine twice insists that melody in verse must come before all else:

"De la musique avant toute chose" . . . . . .

and again:

"De la musique encore, et toujours".

As this poet, sad and remorseful, sat at his prison window and contemplated the calm blue sky beyond the bars, he had no regard, I think, for the obscurities of language any more, and — as must naturally occur when the emotions are deeply stirred — expresses his regrets in the most simple and lovely language imaginable, ending with the heart-rending cry:

> *"Qu'as-tu fait, ô toi que voilà,*
> *Pleurant sans cesse,*
> *Dis, qu'as-tu fait, toi que voilà,*
> *De ta jeunesse?"*

I think sometimes that the art of poetry has reached its apogee, that what has been done can possibly be equalled, but not surpassed. The bulk of what has emerged in modern times, the prosaic and often boring personal statements that one strives to understand, are outside the legitimate avenues of poetry as we have known it through our glorious centuries. They are not poetry in its highest sense. It is indeed difficult to depart from the customary rules of the poetic art, from the essentials that make it a thing other than prose. The main essential, as I have already tried to express, is melody, the music of words; and that music will be compounded of many elements, of which not the least — in addition to a happy choice of words and phrase, which quality enriches the poetry of Dylan Thomas — are alliteration and repetition and rhyme. These ornaments of poetry are not consciously and deliberately chosen. They come naturally in the outflow of a poet's thoughts and feelings. They are the sort of music that is inherent in Nature, in the ebb and flow of the tide, in the burden of a song. The great blank verse lines of Shakespeare, the soliloquies especially, though unrhymed, owe their musical beauty very largely to the inclusion of the elements of which I have spoken. And these elements are all apparent in the wild and stirring charm of the irregular chants of Walt Whitman, and in the English translation of the Psalms.

I cannot tell you of all my companions, as I would wish, but we formed a circle, in the recent past, that was unusual and happy; and I believe that in the lovely Inn tensions were eased, and people emerged as their true and best selves. I remember the ladies, among them Audrey and Deirdre and Frances, and Jane and Anne — the names "five sweet symphonies", like the names of the ladies in Rosetti's "Blessed Damozel". There was a fragrance of personality there, and it lingers still.

Sometimes in the evening I am on the point of leaving the inn, on account of the pressure of customers and a feeling of claustrophobia, of being hemmed in, when of a sudden the standing figures become a more cohesive group, and begin to sing. I am in the presence of a magnificent choir.

The human voice is to me the sweetest of music. I would love to be able to sing, but, alas, I have no voice. My father sang well in a tenor voice, my great-uncle Tom too, and indeed quite a number of my relations, ladies on his side especially, were notable singers. Uncle Tom was invited often from his fishing-boat at the Barbican in Plymouth to sing at concerts ashore. As an old man, when we brought some tobacco to him in his cottage at Mousehole, he could be persuaded to sing once more his two favourite pieces of music — "The Dear Little Shamrock" and a religious hymn that was a great favourite: "He wipes the tear from every eye".

At our home in Mousehole — my brother at the piano accompanying her — I heard my cousin Emmie sing for the first time. It was a practice for a song she was to sing at a concert in the School Hall. These concerts were a feature of our village life in those days, simple and enjoyable entertainments. My cousin had a lovely voice. The shyness we had expected at the outset was not apparent to us at all. She sang, as we used to say, "like a thrush", and later was for many years a member of the Wesleyan Chapel Choir, a group of singers of unusual talent.

As I listen to the magnificent choir I have no longer any thoughts of departure. The Inn is now vibrant with song, and I am strangely moved. I hear a powerful and sweet soprano voice, and strong bass notes which, I think, come from a burly man furthest from me, across the room. But no, I am amazed when I realise that they proceed from a small, frail-looking young man with a beard in the centre of the group. How is it possible, I wonder, for a small man like that to be capable of such deep and resonant tones?

I listen to the Cornish voices, and go out, later, into the shadow of the church, and the strains reach me still as I go down the dark lane to my home in Penolva valley.

Sometimes too, of an evening, the curtains of the saloon part, and from across the village green come a troupe of players — the Saint Pol de Léon Players, fresh from their rehearsals in the Church Hall. A rosy apple-faced girl trips forth. She is small, remarkably vivacious, absorbed still in her part, and as she sings with her companions the whole house responds, in the soft subdued light.

There is surprising ability in these players. The lady who has directed them brilliantly in their several performances slips in quietly, usually last, modestly eclipsing herself. It is remarkable how this Inn has become the centre of so much that is artistic and intellectual.

As I sit there, especially at night, I am conscious of the beautiful church behind me, just outside the bared granite walls. The great tower is so close that if it fell it would flatten the Inn. Never, I think, could the placing of Church and hostelry have been more happily conceived. I begin to wonder how long their companionship has lasted. Perhaps there was always an Inn here, to which the builders of the tower retired for refreshment, centuries ago, when they would make all sorts of excuses to persuade their employers to release them for a while. It is a fact, of course, that these towers often took years — in the case of cathedrals perhaps ten years to complete. The work proceeded in stages, since hasty building would endanger the safety of the structure. The weather was perhaps softer and sunnier in those days, sometime before 1500 A.D., when the tower was built, so that after hoisting their flag, or perhaps a green branch, as was the custom, to indicate to their employer that a break was due — some portion of wall or buttress having been completed — they would cross over to the Inn for a short respite, and look wonderingly down the rough narrow road to Mouzel and the lovely blue spreading bay.

This Inn was to me, in imagination, as a boy, the "Admiral Benbow" of "Treasure Island", for the events related in that wonderful story could well have had their setting here; and some of the frequenters of the Inn whom I knew reminded me, weirdly, of those desperate pirates of old.

There was "Old Carey", as we knew him, a retired naval man, I think, who lodged at the Inn, and whom we saw, frequently, reeking of alcohol, making uncertain strides to and from the Inn whilst cursing us "dêm boys". He could well have been the Blind Beggar tapping along towards the Inn to deliver the "black spot" to Billy Jones, the much-feared Captain who would demand silence, and terrify the customers.

There was indeed a "Captain" I knew at a later time, who sat in the corner of the Inn, by the fire, with his pint of beer. A lovely old chap, very quiet, a great contrast to the terrible Bones, but who nevertheless expected to be addressed as "Captain". He certainly did not demand silence, but occasionally, and quite unexpectedly, when his pint glass had been replenished for the last time, would break into song, and entertain us with extracts from "The Mikado", or another of Gilbert and Sullivan's operas, which he seemed to know from beginning to end. A look of contentment would spread over his rounded face as he sang. It was a prelude to his departure, late enough for him to go and peer into the adjacent lounge, where his wife, observing his presence, would make no demur in accepting what was in fact a demand, and accompany him homewards, down towards the Moor and their little cottage by the stream.

I did not see any real pirates in the narrow bar reeking with smoke in the old days when Walter Carne, Dick Nicholls, Johnny Perry and their boon companions settled before a coal fire for their game of euchre; but I did have at times related to me, as a younger man, and sotto voce, stories of smuggling — by perpetrators of that strangely alluring business themselves — of illicit exchanges in the darkness somewhere between Brest and the Merlin Rock. And I was told — and have since almost forgotten — that the greatest profit was not in spirits, but in silks. Even as I was listening to these tales, a Preventive Officer entered from his little hut over the hedge nearby, and mingled unsuspectingly with his companions.

It is a long time now since smuggling was common practice in Cornwall, especially along our southern coast. Lacking sufficient knowledge, I cannot give any true account of it myself, but I seem to have a link with it somehow, a sort of inherited sympathy with those adventurers into the dark; a wicked feeling that I would have engaged in the nefarious business myself.

Mr. Hamilton Jenkin, in his book entitled "Cornish Seafarers" gives an interesting and comprehensive picture of smuggling in Cornwall from very early days, but especially during the eighteenth century, when he concludes that it had reached "the zenith of its prosperity". It is alarming to read in his book that even the eventual arming of the Preventive Officers had little impact upon the daring of the smugglers, who operated in fast sailing vessels, armed craft often, reaching up to two or three hundred tons burden. These vessels were owned by wealthy farmers or well-to-do landed gentry, who paid regular wages and arranged for the efficient distribution of the contraband goods. And, such was the sympathetic link between the smugglers and the shore folk, that the officers of the law were quite powerless at times to carry out their duties. Intimidation was rife, and bloodshed frequent, and juries afraid to convict. In fact, it was even possible at times to land goods quite openly, in daylight. Safety lay in numbers, so many were engaged in the trade.

It is amusing to read, In Mr. Jenkin's book, how, during one daylight landing in Mousehole, where smuggling was rife, the local exciseman kept to his bed in fear, "having been pelted with stones a few days before". And even the Mayor of Penzance was "bound over" to refrain from smuggling, under threat of a heavy fine.

The smuggling trade declined towards the end of last century, but still lingered in the extreme west of Cornwall, where fishermen put out on dark nights to meet their Breton accomplices, say from the notorious port of Roscoff, near Brest, and transfer the illicit and valuable cargo to their own boats. These cargoes consisted in the main of spirits — brandy and rum — silks, tobacco and lace.

It is a fact that smuggling in those days was regarded more or less as a legitimate trade; indeed one could almost say a necessary trade, because of the extreme poverty of the fishermen and the miners. Strict Methodists, otherwise men of impeccable character, had no scruples to prevent them engaging in the practice. Even the influence of John Wesley, whose sermons, whether at Gwennap Pit or elsewhere in Cornwall, had a tremendous religious impact upon the people, failed to deter them from a trade which was, as they thought, fair, contributing, as it undoubtedly did, to their physical welfare.

II
The Church. Change and Decay.

Let me now leave the Inn for a while and enter the magic cave of the Church, passing from the noise and bustle of the outside world into the arresting hush of the interior. There is a feeling of solidity here, and amplitude. The hexagonal granite pillars, with their roughly wrought capitals, stand firm and solid. And fortunately, for me at least, there is no rood-screen to interrupt the long, satisfying sweep of the nave towards the East. I have never understood why in so many churches that long sweep is interrupted in such a manner as to almost shut from view the glorious blaze of the eastern window.

It is well know that this church was partially destroyed by raiding Spaniards in 1595. There are differing opinions as to how much destruction was actually wrought upon that occasion. It is hard to believe that what fire there was could have destroyed the huge stone pillars of the interior. It might have been that the original pillars were so damaged and marked by the fire that they had to be removed and replaced. Some authorities state that the present pillars were there at the time of the fire; others, however, that they were erected after the fire, and that their present inclination towards the north and south has been due solely to inferior workmanship. It is a difficult and intriguing problem, and I have not been able from the little I have read to solve it to my own satisfaction.

The pillars do not seem to sustain a very heavy burden; and if any subsidence had occurred it would surely have resulted in a certain regularity of slant. But no, they seem to be truly in line. The problem deepens, and one is tempted to ask if they were actually built like that, if there were some unexplained constructional reason for erecting them as they appear today, but this I can scarcely credit. The foundations of the Tower itself must of necessity have been dug deep — reaching solid rock — and there is no visible disturbance of its bulk. I think probably the same care was not observed in the case of the pillars, and that subsidence did actually occur. In any case some opposite pillars are now strapped together with steel bars, in an effort to prevent any further outward thrust.

It is interesting to me to have noticed that in certain foundations being dug quite nearby white clay was encountered at no great depth. It would not be surprising if a layer of this were spread over quite a large area, extending to the base of the Church itself, forming a somewhat insecure platform for building, and a reason, perhaps, for the shifting and inclination of the pillars. There is a similar inclination of the pillars in the church at St. Ives, though slighter, and in other churches in the district.

Behind the pulpit there is a narrow arch, supported by two shafts carrying capitals of unusual design. They are of limestone, kept, it seems, deliberately, after the fire, and showing marks of the same; suggesting, incidentally, that in the mediaeval church that was here, before granite came gradually to be used in the interiors, the shafts and capitals must have been of limestone, and more elaborately wrought than was possible with granite. I think the church then must have been even more beautiful than it is now.

Most of the Cornish churches have piers of granite, and indeed, as they stand, massively, one could claim that they are a true reflection of the rugged Cornish landscape and the character of its people. Nevertheless, I would like to have seen Paul Church with its limestone pillars, soft to the gaze, in the evening light.

The Normans brought huge quantities of limestone by sea from their great quarries at Caen, in Normandy. It was a good building stone, especially for interiors, but apt to crumble somewhat in the damp atmosphere of the West. This might account for the curious lack of Norman workmanship in our County. It is probable that the interior walls of churches in Cornwall were of granite from quite early on after the Conquest. The Normans sought out limestone quarries in several places in the South West, which, more especially perhaps at Beer in South Devon, provided material for the limestone piers which, in the Gothic style later, adorn many of our churches today. I am thinking of the churches at St. Just, St. Ives, Madron, St. Keverne, and others. The intricate moulding of the capitals in these churches could scarcely have been achieved in granite, although it is startling to see what has been accomplished in that respect in the beautiful churches of St. Buryan and Ludgvan.

I have mentioned the church at St. Just, where the piers are of limestone, brought probably from Beer. The walls of this church, as in some others, have been bared of plaster, to reveal the original granite, and deep-pointed with great skill in this particular instance. The bareness has revealed the great skill of the original builders. You see it all now in the rough — the magnificent placing of the stones, especially in the window embrasures and the arches, and you might feel that there was never any necessity to cover it up at all, that it is more beautiful as it is, this church; that the bared stone has given it austerity, a greater silence, a monastic charm.

I have spoken a lot of granite, the granite that I have always loved, and of the difficulty of moulding it to shape. Well, there is a granite here in West Cornwall called "Ludgvan granite". It comes from a quarry at Ludgvan. It is a sparkling granite, sparkling with mica, and somewhat finer grained at times, and easier to carve, than most of our local granite. It is rather beautiful, and special. So it seems to have been used for special purposes in the past. You see it in the lovely font in St. Levan Church — of Norman work, unusual for granite at that period — in the font also at

St. Ives, of much more recent date; in the piers at Ludgvan; in the porch surround at Paul; and in the window surrounds at the Old Standard in Mousehole. You will see it with its sparkle in many other places, the lovely Ludgvan granite.

I have wandered away from the church at Paul and I must return. I have not been a worshipper there in a congregational sense for a long time; but often, and alone, I have entered into the same hushed, holy silence as when, a boy, on Sundays, I entered the lower door, wonderingly. Something holds me back from a closer connection with its services. It is partly that I felt attendance there had become too much of a formality; but mainly, I think, that in my broad acceptance of the teaching of Jesus I could not bring myself to embrace some of the traditional Christian beliefs. However, to me, the service is beautiful, and I would hate to see it altered.

There can be great danger in change. And it is very sad when something that is beautiful is changed to something that is ugly and commonplace. Having read many extracts of the so-called "New Bible", I cannot cease to wonder why there had to be any change at all. Was it assumed that people were so ignorant that they could not understand the original renderings? If so it were a grievous error. The folks of my day, and especially the old people, understood the Bible all right. They **lived** by it. So why had it to be re-written?

There is a wonderful short story in the Authorised Version of the Bible — the story of the Prodigal Son, a story couched in simple and magnificent language; perhaps the best short story ever written. And they have changed even that! I do not really know who "they" are, or by what authority they have presumed to alter something which is not theirs.

I must now give some instances of the changes that have been made. To give many would be quite unnecessary, because what has been done will be quite apparent from the few I have chosen. I mentioned above the story of the Prodigal Son and the beauty of the language in which it was told. In that story the following changes occur:

"The portion of goods that falleth to me" becomes "Give me my share of the property". "Wasted his substance with riotious living" becomes "Squandered it in reckless living". "He began to be in want" becomes "He began to feel the pinch". "He fain would have filled his belly with the husks that the swine did eat" becomes "He would have been glad to fill his belly with the pods that the pigs were eating". And "No man gave unto him" becomes "No man gave him anything".

What is the purpose of this rubbish? What conclave of clerics or laity or dons could have sat down to perpetrate these weak and totally unnecessary substitutions? They do not like, apparently, the quaint traditional character of certain words, the force, the striking impact of the original.

What is in the stars they have brought down to common earth. In probing too closely into the meanings, which are already clear enough, in engaging in a sort of dissection, as it were, they have taken away the colour, the enamel, the glory. I am reminded of certain lines of the poet John Keats in his poem "Lamia", in which he suggests that all charms could fly at what he calls "cold philosophy" — the word "philosophy" being at that time a term for "Natural Science":

> "There was an awful rainbow once in heaven:
> We know her woof, her texture; she is given
> In the dull catalogue of common things.
> Philosophy will clip an Angel's wings."

The "dull catalogue" of the "New Bible" is continued in the mutilation of Corinthians 13, where, among other things, the word "love" is substituted for the beautiful and more all-embracing word "charity".

"And now abideth faith, hope and charity, these three;" must give place to the miserable alternative: "In a word, there are three things that last for ever, faith, hope and love".

The result of the above changes is that the whole beauty of the passage is lost.

I must add here that just recently, attending the funeral service of the wife of one of my boyhood companions, I was appalled, as I listened to the reading from the New Bible, at the mutilation of this passage, which had gone much further than I would have thought possible. The whole structure of the quite lucid and beautiful edifice was impaired. Why, I cannot conceive.

I have not sufficient knowledge to comment on the changes occurring in the Book of Common Prayer, which I believe are much resented; but I have seen a modern rendering of the Lord's Prayer which is included, and which reduces the simple and glorious utterance to a banality that appals.

It has been customary, through the centuries, in addressing our prayers and petitions to the God whom Christians acknowledge and worship, to use the singular pronouns "Thou" and "Thee" and "Thy", as befitting a Majesty and Presence before which we stand in awe. How sad, therefore, to see the alacrity with which so many ministers of religion accept the ugly modern "You", reducing in the process the Majesty above us to something of mere flesh and blood. I wonder if the striking significance of the word "which" in the Lord's Prayer has ever been apparent to these ministers. It is a pronoun wonderfully chosen, relating to something great and good, beyond our understanding, out of the confines of our physical world.

I have spoken of the beauty of the Biblical language, and of the mutilations that have occurred. It may be that some readers of this little book which I hope to complete sometime will think that I have exaggerated the case for the importance of language. I think not. The astonishing beauty of the language in the Authorised Version stems from, is a result of, the intensity of religious feeling of the early translators. It is great language that moves. Let the glorious utterances, therefore, be presented intact to aspiring youth, and not supplanted — at the whim of some well-meaning, but unappreciative cleric — by language that is common and devoid of beauty.

I doubt if considerations of doctrine are powerfully present often in the minds of young people. What then, for them, are the things that could inspire and uplift as they follow tradition and continue to attend the church services? I believe that they are — and I try to put them in order of importance — the beauty of the church itself (and many of our English churches are very beautiful); the magnificence of the traditional language; and, finally, the ability of the minister to speak with power, to give force to the striking passages, to impress by the depth and sincerity of his thoughts.

I mount several beautifully-carved stone steps and pass through a rather lovely gate into the churchyard. The gate is one of several placed in memory of a gentleman much respected in the village, a bell-ringer and connected with the sea. The iron structure is an intricate and pleasing pattern of anchors and bells.

Steps and Gate into Churchyard at Paul, by Stanhope Forbes

I stand in the churchyard, among the twisted and sunken memorials. There is a strange silence over this field of death, where I am the only living soul. I read the inscriptions on the tombs, the tributes paid, the solid faith, the confident hopes expressed by those who mourned their dead; and I feel small.

The elms that once shaded the churchyard are now bare, having been unable to resist the terrible disease that has destroyed so many thousands of them in our countryside. The tracery of their branches is beautiful, especially in the light cast upon them at night; but they drip sadness in the soft, moist air, and soon the dreaded note of the chain saw will be heard, and they will be seen no more.

Not far from the doomed trees are some of our Cornish elms, which seem to be unaffected by the killer disease, and stand in full bloom alongside their unhappy companions.

Fortunately, many sycamores remain, the lovely trees which are not native to our country, having been introduced from the Continent some centuries ago. They grow rapidly, attaining to full stature in a matter of fifty or sixty years, and are well established among us. If only the authorities could be persuaded to plant more and more of these beautiful trees!

There is, across the village green, behind the old school building, now the Church Hall, another place of rest, and if you go up through it to the end, you arrive at a very peaceful and lovely spot indeed — a wonderful sort of elevated green platform, thrust out somewhat above the near fields, and open to the blue bay. Beneath the sycamores it is lit happily in the morning light as the sun comes up over what we call our "Eastern Land". Here lie many of quite recent date, and some who became closer and dearer to me because of the lady who became my wife.

I hope that the headstones which have been placed on the surface of the narrow path leading to this quiet and lovely spot will be removed. They came from the old portion of the graveyard which had become very much overgrown; but many of them are records of people who can be presently remembered, and one hopes that some permission for their removal had been sought. In any case, if they have been legitimately removed, they could well have been placed against the boundary walls, as in the old "cholera ground" at Paul, and in many other graveyards. Then this stepping over memorials, this macabre journey to the end peaceful haven could have been avoided, and the path could have been surfaced with an effective and attractive sort of decomposed felspar we call "rabb".

Another resting place is not so far away, and there lie many whom I have loved, some very close to me, my own relations, among them one who gave me life, my own Mother, to whose nobility I feel I could never attain. I wish that some happy day I could see them all again.

I have mentioned the old cholera-ground at Paul, which has remained somewhat of a mystery to many people. Cholera had spread westwards from Asiatic countries in 1830, and had affected many places in Cornwall, especially the seaports, which harboured vessels from all over the world. Newlyn was a special victim, and so many died of the disease there that an extra burial ground was needed. A meadow separate from the church was donated by the Lord of the Manor, James Halse. That meadow became what we always called, as boys, the "Cholera Ground". We imagined that it was more ancient than it actually was, but if we had read the memorials carefully I think we should have found that the dates were mostly from 1830 onwards.

The West Briton of those times recorded that the cholera was so severe at Newlyn that the Mousehole inhabitants "established a quarantine", and prohibited any Newlyn person from entering their village. This added fire to whatever traditional antagonisms already existed between the two vilages, and the Newlyn folk — the epidemic having subsided there — retorted in kind, and declared that no Mousehole person should move through their village. One can imagine the impact of this upon the stout fishers of Mousehole. Their attempt to defy the edict was met with stones and any weapons at hand, but after a particularly vicious encounter they were forced to retire.

The siting of the village of Paul is unique. From it, like the fingers of a hand, roads and narrow lanes stretch out in many directions across the mysterious land that is Penwith. The existence of that land, and of the misty islands beyond, the Cassiterrides of old, the throb of it, is here, in this village of Paul, palpable, even if the surf against the Logan Rock, and the Longships, and the Brisons, and the sighing of the dreaded Runnelstone, are not actually heard. Something from the long past is over it, the persisting echo, perhaps, of great happenings, glorious deeds of momentous import, long, long ago.

I have called this land mysterious, and that it has been to me always, acquainted with it as I have been from my boyhood. Upon others too, and many, has fallen its spell, the spell of Penwith.

"When I came back from Lyonesse,
   With magic in my eyes"

wrote Hardy, drawn there from "a hundred miles away". Was it the misted land across the water that held him in awe? Did he hear the church bells ringing in the sunken parishes? Was it by day that he stood in wonder, or in the night, when the great cliffs were a presence felt, and the Wolf and Longships Lights lit the waters?

The Longships
High on a granite rock I stand,
Between the Scillies and the land,
You can hear the sullen roar
Of my breakers from the shore,
You can hear the nearer moan
Of the dreadful Runnelstone,
And the thunder of the foam
On the Brisons driven home,
While at your feet, and evermore,
The gulls above the surges soar.
I am a beacon in the night,
Out of the Darkness cometh Light.

III
Down the Lane to Mousehole

Before I leave the village of Paul, and go down the lane to Mousehole where I was born, eighty-six years ago now, I have something to relate. Among the visitors to the Inn there was a gentleman from London who had spent many a holiday in this part of Cornwall, and who was never happier than when he had crossed the Tamar and come to stay with his friends in Newlyn. His enthusiasm for West Cornwall knew no bounds. Rain mattered not to him; no adverse condition of the elements could damp his spirits, so long as he was here, where he longed to be.

Basil had a great influence upon me. He wanted me to put into writing what little knowledge I still retained of Paul and Mousehole in the old days. He pestered me. How could I, an old man, summon up the energy and inspiration to do the thing he wished for me? His insistence worried me, and indeed at times I was at pains to avoid the enquiries he would assuredly make as to the progress I had made in that matter of writing which he had urged me to.

There are smouldering fires in me, and Basil fanned them into flame. I had for a very long time had it in my thoughts to do what he wanted me to do; and I had now arrived at the point when failure to set about the task in real earnest would mean very much more to me than to him.

It is, nevertheless, with tremulous fingers that I enter upon a task which, before my dormant enthusiasms had been awakened, I would have thought to be quite beyond my powers.

I have a brother who wrote an absorbing and beautifully set out tale of the villages of Paul and Mousehole, some aspects of which I shall try to recapture; and I ask myself often what I can add to what he has written, and written so well. There is also "A Short History of Mousehole, with Personal Recollections", a comprehenisve and interesting book, written by Nettie Mann Pender, who died a few years ago.

Comprehensive as have been the books I have mentioned, I feel that there are omissions, that there is a lot more to be said, especially of the boats, the magnificent luggers, the fine, dignified, intelligent race of fishermen, and the life they led.

So, more adventurously than I had dreamed possible, I go down now towards Mousehole, down the lane that was so quiet and beautiful when I was a boy. The blackthorns and hawthorns in the hedges were cut back lovingly then, not brutally, their beauty unassailed by the destroying claws of modern machines; and there were many trees, especially sycamores, that had no fear in those days of so-called "tree surgeons" or the dreaded note of the chain saw. There were those who used the "hook", with long-acquired and remarkable skill, and never a stone was ripped rashly from the hedges then.

A horse, asserting itself, rebelling for a moment, would hesitate in the shafts and stretch for the more inviting tufts of grass; and the driver, perhaps, fond and proud of his charge, would relax for a while, in sleepy content. The tempo of life was deliciously slow. Was it not just as lovely then, this lane, with the same sea-breath upon it, the same stirring of the senses as the one leading down to Breffny, so beloved of Eva Gore-Booth?

It has retained a certain beauty, this little lane, even to this day. It is to be hoped that it will never be widened, never straightened; that gradually there will be greater control — which up to now has been, very wrongly, neglected — over the speed of its traffic, which is alarming and very dangerous indeed at times.

The beauty of approach is a feature of the fishing villages of Cornwall. I think of Newlyn, especially, at the moment, where a pleasant walk, parallel to the seaward road, has been contrived for walkers down the beautiful Coombe. It is to be hoped that there will be little change there, that the speculative intentions of intruders unresponsive to its beauty will be strenuously resisted. I hope that there will always be some strong artistic element in the constitution of the Penwith Council, to ensure that the approach to Newlyn remains beautiful.

Two or three hundred yards below the Church at Paul, a narrow road, on the left, hidden until one is almost upon it, goes down to a lovely little valley. There is a stream, bridged in two places with granite stones, and a pond, from which, sadly, the ducks have been absent for a long time now. One duck did come to it quite recently — a white duck with a red beak, of a species unknown to me. It was probably fatigued after a long flight, and was, indeed, quite tame. One day it was off again on its journey, and we saw it no more.

The valley I speak of is the valley of Penolva. It has been beloved of many, this quiet little hollow, so unexpectedly discovered, so close to the village of Mousehole. And many artists, responsive to its charm, have set up their easels here. Such an artist was Stanhope Forbes, who has left us in his paintings a comprehensive and faithful story of West Cornwall, the places he loved, the people he loved and felt for; and, happily, in colours that one can see and understand. He painted a delightful picture of Penolva, just as it was in the beginning of the century. You see the pool where the ducks once swam, the little bridges over the stream, the outhouses, the old dead cart with the grey horse, "Lucy", in the "sharps", the figure of a man on top of the load — possibly of trimmings from the hedges — and a woman, his wife, perhaps, standing by.

The old horse worked for my neighbour Raymond and his father years ago when they ran this farm at Penolva and the one at Gwavas. She was 30 years old when Raymond summoned up the courage to put her to sleep, his father then too fond to perform the necessary act.

Penolva, by Stanhope Forbes

Other pictures of Stanhope Forbes could formerly be seen in the Passmore Edwards Art Gallery at Newlyn. Upon calling there a little while ago and finding none, I was told by the lady at the desk — and regretfully — that they had been removed to the Mayor's Parlour at St. John's Hall, Penzance. I hope that it is only a temporary arrangement, and that they will soon be returned to the Gallery.

The name "Passmore Edwards" is engraved in granite on the facade of that Gallery. That is its traditional title, and many would wish it to remain so, wondering why it has suddenly and unaccountably become the "Orion", a pretentious and unsuitable appellation.

There was an extensive orchard here at Penolva once, when the Carnes lived in the old farmhouse, and I am afraid that for us boys the codlings were too much of a temptation. The apple trees have all gone, the last few lonely ones unable to stand the ferocity of a recent gale which laid them low. Recently what is now an attractive sloping meadow then was brilliant and beautiful with anemones.

Further down the lane from the Penolva turn is a cottage on the right, secluded — the spot chosen for that reason — now occupied by a noted lady artist. The cottage was built many years ago by a great friend of my family, Olaf Baker, a writer of boys' books, including one which I remember: "Shasta of the Wolves". Olaf was a clever writer, a lover of peace and quiet. Quiet above all. I can recall that he once lived in a cottage behind the Inn at Paul which was demolished by a bomb during the last war. He was certainly not alone in his desire for quiet, but even the occasional braying of a donkey in the adjacent meadow was a painful disturbance to him. I am not at all sure that the lovely, and innocent, animal was not the reason for his departure from that cottage next to the stile and the fields leading into Trevithal.

Olaf had a quaint old gipsy caravan. Where he got it from I cannot say. He pitched it among the sea-pinks and heather somewhere on the cliff top close to the beautiful Kynance Cove, I stayed there with him for a few days once. Delightfully quiet it was — just the song of the birds, the humming of bees, the rustling heather, the murmur of the sea. There must be many, I think, in these days of universal and raucous noise, who long to escape for a while, too, to a similar place of peace; whose thoughts turn from some turbulent London, such as the poet Yeats knew, to some peaceful Innisfree.

A peaceful isle a poet sighed for,
As I do too;
I see more beauty in the old
Than in the new;
I wish the skies were uninvaded,
That only birds were flying there,
In their own established places,
In the free, unfettered air.
I trust that there will still be islands,
Actual, and of the mind,
Quiet places, just like this,
For which the Irish poet pined.

    The cottage Olaf built was occupied later, for some years, by a lady artist named Miss Bruford. I cannot give an opinion of her as a painter, but I do remember her as an engagingly eccentric lady. She brought with her from "up country", as we say, down here, two pet ravens which flew freely about the valley. She possessed also a pathetic little monkey which loved to sit upon her shoulders, accompanying her in her walks.
    The direct descendants of those two ravens are in the valley still, and their deep croaks can often be heard, shorter and more raucous than the note of the carrion crows which, seen rarely and only in pairs here some years ago, are now far more numerous, even quite common, especially in the nesting season, when they wait in the branches, sinister bundles, for favourable moments to do their nefarious, if natural work.
    My near neighbour in the valley first came here from Gwavas in 1912, the year of the terrible Titanic disaster. His knowledge of the birds around has always been considerable, and it is he who told me about the ravens, including in his story a most interesting and striking occurrence. The ravens built, he said, always, in one of the elm trees bordering his orchard field, and reconstituted their nest, the same nest, year after year. Came one year when that particular nest was abandoned, and the ravens built in an adjoining tree — in response, perhaps, to an instinct, a prescience unknown, lost, to us; for, only a few days after, the old tree had fallen, and lay athwart the stream, prone.
    The lady artist, Ithell Colquhoun, who now lives in Olaf's cottage, paints there and writes there, contentedly, so long as her little garden is quiet. She crosses the river sometimes and comes up to us, especially if she is disturbed by artificial and unnecessary noise. She comes then, perhaps, for the sort of comfort that can be obtained when fellow-sufferers meet. For I suffer also from excessive, unnatural noise, intensely so, along with many who are gentle enough not to offend, not to cause ill will by protestations that in reality should be made. For the countryside is not so peaceful as it was. The quiet that once obtained, that was for many a

dream, a basic necessity, is often sought in vain. I think the worst shatterer of that quiet is the so-called "bird scarer", which can produce a succession of deafening explosions — vastly more disturbing than anything from Concorde — over a whole winter period, at intervals sometimes of only a few minutes. It is indeed an unwarranted intrusion, a thing to be feared. Farmers, of course, have to protect their cabbages, and quite a few, I am sure, are feeling enough to see to it that the intervals between the explosions are reasonably long, say ten minuts at least. There are machines which emit sounds inaudible to humans, but audible to birds, which, I have read, are quite effective, and which, used, would be an inestimable boon to many.

At the bottom of Ithell's garden is a little gate, and steps leading down to the road. And across the road was once what was known to us as "the Monument". It marked the spot where a murder was committed, nearly two hundred years ago. Martha Blewett, an old woman of Mousehole, was robbed and murdered by a young fisherman, William Trewavas, aged 26, on her way to Paul Church. A granite monument erected on the spot bore the following inscription:

> "Oh remember the Almighty,
> The great King of Kings and
> Lord of Lords: Hath in the
> table of his law commanded
> Thou shalt do no murder."

William Trewavas was arrested, tried at Launceston, found guilty, and executed for his crime in 1793. The monument was dismantled many years ago now, but the flat dressed-granite stones which formed it have been incorporated into the hedge, and can still be seen. For years it was regarded as an eerie experience, and to be feared, to pass that memorial on the way up the lane, especially at night, from Mousehole to Paul.

A few yards farther down the lane from the site of the Monument there is a slight widening of the road, where, not so many years ago, there was a gate. Right down close to the road, a granite stone — one of the larger ones which normally form the basis of our Cornish hedges — bears the chiselled inscription:

> C.T.
> 1887

It was the year of Queen Victoria's Golden Jubilee, and my father, Charles Tregenza, chiselled it as he came down with his hammer and cold chisels from some job up in the countryside. I love to imagine him, a powerful young man then of 24, a builder — as was his father and grandfather before him — stopping here, doing a bit each day until the lettering was complete. It was well chiselled, too. And the chisels were sharp and kept their edge much longer than those of today. They were expertly tempered in the forge at Sheffield, just above Paul Village, or in the forge near the old bridge at Newlyn.

The Harvey boys, with their father, worked the forge at Sheffield in the early part of the century. It was wonderful to us as boys inside that forge — the metallic atmosphere, the smeechy smell of the place, the quickening of the coals from red to almost white, magically, under the blower, the clang of the anvil, the skilful shapings, the deft strokes. And the blacksmiths loomed as gods. Outside, horses waited patiently to be "shoed", yielding up their legs eventually to be clasped tightly between the knees of the smith. The reek of the smoking hooves is in my nostrils still.

We had iron hoops, with drills, in those days, and took them when broken to the forge to be "scarfed". As we did at Mousehole too, when we were still younger. The forge there was in a small building facing the harbour, where now sand has been placed for children to play; and the blacksmith was named "Harvey", too.

I realise that I am moving slowly down the lane towards Mousehole, and I must hurry, lest I am overtaken by events that will make it impossible for me to complete my story. I go down a little further than my father's chiselled memorial, and on the left a narrow little road leads into "Lynwood", perhaps the most pleasantly situated house in Mousehole. I think it was built by a member of the Victor family — a relative of my boyhood friend, Herbert Victor, whose little water colours of local scenes are so popular with visitors — more than a hundred years ago. We lived there for a short time ourselves when I was about ten years old. Before that I remember there was a Museum there, known as Bailey's Museum. I cannot remember all the things the retired doctor displayed there, but I do know that there were stuffed birds and animals, and that the Museum was open to the public. Also that he had an electric organ, and that there was a beautiful eucalyptus in the garden. He lived in style, sporting a carriage and pair, and a coachman. A Dr. Duncan lived there later, and Doctor Enid Smith. Mary Duncan, a talented artist, one of Dr. Duncan's daughters, came back there to spend her last years when it was a home for old people, run by my brother Alan and his wife Vera. Two lovely pictures by Mary Duncan face me now on our walls as I write.

During the first world war a group of Belgian women refugees found a temporary home there in "Lynwood".

On the other side of the road into Lynwood a group of houses forming the pleasant estate called "Parc-an-Gate" stand where once there was a lovely orchard, owned by the Waters family of Mousehole. They were skilful market gardeners, and owned most of the meadows either side of the lane leading to Paul. They grew daffodils, Scilly Whites, Soleil d'ors, violets in those meadows, and the flowers were picked by girls from the village, who formed a happy band always, even though the wages the growers could afford to give were small indeed in those days.

The Waters had cows, too, and I remember slicing mangolds for them in the cowshed which stood where now there are two or three garages.

I walk in wonder now, for, magically, down there in the gaps between the houses, upon the water, it is surely an island that appears. Like a sprawling lion it unfolds: a massive paw, defiantly placed — that is the "Shag Rock". Another, the left paw, its fellow — that is the rock by the "Leaden". Shaggy shoulders rearing up — that is "Carn Luge". The long tawny back — that is the centre, the level stretch, where sea-pinks, once, and grasses, grew. The tufted tail — that is the rock we called the "Gull Rock". And the proud lion at last, in its entirety — St. Clement's Island.

I have always stood in wonder at the shape of that island, a quarter of a mile from the shore, protector of the village from the south-east gales. It is uncannily beautiful. The granite headlands of Penwith, especially the imposing mass of the Logan Rock, have the same disturbing beauty, the same unlikely contour, the same symmetry that is no symmetry at all. It is as though some inspired giant from the past had chiselled them out, with skill beyond our understanding, and made them beautiful.

St. Clement's Island

Placed upon the highest point of St. Clement's Island is a stone pillar, which is really a mark of ownership.

My uncle Herbert, cousin Vaughan's father, kept a wonderful diary, and in that diary there is a most interesting account of the placing of that stone, written, in a magnificent hand, in 1890. I think I cannot do better, as I go along, than to use his own words. Here is what he wrote:

"In October, 1890, Mr. Bolitho (Thos. B.) had a stone cut, and his name placed thereon, dated back to the time 1869, when he became Lord of the Manor, claiming with it the Island title. He desired to have this stone put on the top of the present base of stone, placed there by the former claimant, Mr. Halse.

"Day was fixed for the job. Poor weather.
All hands stood ready for action, namely,
Mr. John S. Tregenza
Mr. James F. Rowe
Mr. Cherry Maddern
John Grose Trevaskis
Willie Harvey
James Bodinar

"The stone, about 5cwt., was carried on board of punt by hand-barrow, and rested on the thwarts of same — was rowed to the Island by four hands (good oarsmen). Mr. C. Tregenza & Willie were deputed to select landing place, the back of Island being chosen. The boat was hauled up on the rocks by main force (Mr. J.F. Rowe being land mark for oarsmen). The stone was again taken out of the boat, being still on hand-barrow, safe and sound, without an accident to anyone, with the exception that Grose jammed his fingers a little on the gunwale of boat."

The laborious journey to the topmost part of the Island is imaginatively described by my uncle. He represents the heavy stone as being alive, reluctant, resisting, unwilling to be dragged along by its enemies to a spot where it would be exposed to all the fury of the elements.

However, the task was accomplished successfully, and "it was amidst cheers and laughter put in irons, settled on a cold bed of cement. It was left dreary and desolate, to the pity of the elements."

As far as I know, the ownership of St. Clement's island still rests with the Bolitho family.

Stone Pillar on Island

Still further down the lane I pass the old school where my mother taught as a young woman, and where I was a pupil later, with my brothers. It was a fine school, and gave a remarkably good solid basis in most subjects. It was a mark of the excellence of that school. We read from a litle brown book. My wife and I both remember it with gratitude, that little brown book. It was one of the "Royal Readers", and contained extracts from some of our greatest poets. We learnt them by heart — a most valuable exercise which, sad to say, is frowned upon by many educationalists of today. Once having become so familiar, the great passages of our literature are exalting to us always, remain jewels in our remembrance. For, as the young poet Keats says:

"A thing of beauty is a joy forever:
Its loveliness increases, it will never
Pass into nothingness, but still will keep
A bower quiet for us, and a sleep
Full of sweet dreams, and health, and quiet breathing."

There was a fisherman of Mousehole, whom I knew well, and whose intelligence I respected. Intelligence was a mark of the Mousehole fishermen of those times. He could be, in his cups, a little uncomfortable to be with at times; but something would rouse him suddenly in the direction of his thoughts, and Bill — the true Bill, I think — would be uttering words of strange appeal, highly melodious words from the poet Byron and others, words remembered from his boyhood at Mousehole school, which must have occupied a secret, refining place in his mind. I can see him now, for he has gone, turning to me, with a sort of attractive smile, as he spoke the lines, with expression and power:

"There was a sound of revelry by night,
And Belgium's capital had gather'd then
Her Beauty and her Chivalry, and bright
The lamps shone o'er fair women and brave men . . .

"Roll on, thou deep and dark blue Ocean — roll!
Ten thousand fleets sweep over thee in vain;
Man marks the earth with ruin — his control
Stops with the shore . . .

"There is a pleasure in the pathless woods,
There is a rapture on the lonely shore,
There is a society where none intrudes
By the deep Sea, and music in its roar . . ."

Bill had for a moment left the Inn, and moved into the world of Poetry.
How wonderful it is that poetry was taught to us in that little school at Mousehole, that the headmaster was so wise!

IV
The Millpool. Feeling for Granite.

I have come to the little road leading into the Millpool where I was born. It is strange that I cannot remember much of my very early childhood there. The few recollections I have are vivid, though: rocking one of my younger brothers — or possibly my little sister Mary — to sleep in a cradle; my Mother cutting my nails, and combing my hair, for "crawlers"; sleeping three in a bed; fearing to go up the steep stairs to the mysterious attic above.

As we got older, my brothers and I, we went with our companions up a sloping path opposite our house to what we called "The Curtis". I believe "Curters" was the real old name for it, but I cannot be sure. It was an attractive spot, right up against the meadows and the Treen Fields leading to Trevithal. My grandfather had a meadow there, with an apple tree in it. There were lots of elder trees, too — "scaos" we called them. And from the wood of those scaos were made pop-guns — quite a skilful job, really. Looking back, I am astonished at how expert we were in fashioning them. For bullets we chewed newspaper, and, later, used seaweed, which we called "oar-weed", and which gave a much louder and more satisfying report. Of course, we always had good pocket-knives, really good ones, which we could buy at the village stores for sixpence.

The "Curtis" led to an orchard which we seemed to be rather afraid of penetrating, or even to approach. It belonged to a man we called Carey, who lived at the end of a little alley alongside the Salvation Army in Commercial Road in the village. I was never really aware of the relationship between him and the Chirgwin family who lived there too. They stored apples from their orchard there, and sold them, very cheaply. The smell of those apples is in my nostrils still.

On the way up to the Curtis, on the left, was a net loft, owned by the Blewett family, who lived opposite us. They repaired their nets there — a process known as "beeting", and women as well as men would be engaged in this skilful work in lofts all over the village. The Blewett young men were tough, experienced fishermen, and their father was harbour-master at that time. I remember best Frank Blewett ("Nailer"), who was later coxswain of the lifeboat, "The Brothers", and who once allowed me, I remember, later to steer her between the Runnelstone and the land for quite a distance.

There was one year I expect I was about eight years old — when snow appeared for the only time I remember, and carpeted the meadows above the "Curtis". It was very cold, as I thought then. The young Blewetts in the loft spread a net against the hedge of a meadow just next to one owned, or worked, by Jerry Male. It formed a triangular trap for the birds. They closed the ends of this structure; then, at a given moment, with a furious rush, they captured the unhappy half-frozen victims — mainly starlings. It was done when we were young, but it is sad to recall it all.

The road in front of our house was quite spacious, especially at one end, and we played games happily together, boys and girls. We played cutter, catch-mêlée, buck-she-buck, tig, marbles, etc., joining in with the girls in the games more suited to them. At times we played in a little cellar, under Bobby Harvey's house, where there was a lovely smell of nets and ropes, and a swing. It was a long time ago. We were limited, perhaps, in our range of amusements, but we were very inventive, and enjoyed ourselves immensely. There was no vista whatever of the range of diversions available to the children of today.

What shall I say of the remarkably friendly relations that existed between the families in the Millpool? My Mother has spoken of it often — the readiness to help in any sort of trouble, the interest taken in each other's sad and happy times. It was the same throughout the village of Mousehole as in our small enclosure, among the Harveys, the Harrys, the Polgreans, the Ashes, the Pentreaths, the Blewetts, the Trevaskises.

We continued, as boys, to play the game of marbles until we really grew up. It was a skilful game, and some boys were quite expert with their "taws". A shiny taw, taken from a ginger-pop bottle, was a great favourite. We called it a "poopottle". We played "small ring" and, later, "big ring". The "small ring" game would normally reach its conclusion without any untoward occurrence. At times, however, especially if the game had been unduly prolonged, an extraordinary thing could happen. An older boy watching the game might cry, at a given moment, "I can see what this is coming to!", and immediately, to the cry of "Hups! Hups!" there would be a desperate scramble, a frantic effort to "claw up" the remaining marbles in the ring. It was accepted as legitimate! That was the funny thing about it. It makes me laugh now as I recall it. It did not always occur. But when it did it was accepted as legitimate!

I never had any success at that "clawing up", but my brother Walter was pretty good at it. He would be on the floor in a trice at the first warning, clawing desperately in the struggling group, and rarely failed, in any case, to regain his "stakes".

That was the Millpool as I knew it then. A path led up to the Treen Fields, as I have said, and another, rough in those days, but now undamagingly and artistically improved, went up alongside a torrent of a stream to what we called "The Mountains", a delightful little grassy level spot, and eventually to "Betsy Perry's Park", another arcadian enclosure by the river, where we picked blackberries, at the bottom of Trevithal Moor.

A stream ran through the Millpool, crossed by little granite bridges. And, of course, the street was, as a consequence, much more beautiful than it is today, when the bridges we crept venturously under have disappeared, and concrete has covered it all up. Little cobbled paths, beautifully laid, and sometimes patterned, led to the cottage doors through narrow gardens. The cobbles, obtained from the beaches, were just planted in a sort of stiff earth, and today, after so long a time and the tread of so many feet, have lost their curved surfaces and appear quite flat.

Veronicas grew in the gardens then, and their blue flowers were a characteristic feature of the village.

"The Millpool", by Jack Pender

But the veronicas are rarer in the village now, and another lovely plant, the valerian, or setwall, has spread itself irrepressibly in the walls and tumbledown places where the soil is not too rich. This plant is beloved of the Padstow people, and known to them as "Padstow Pride". Until recently, it grew beautiful from the top of a wall leading into the Millpool. It is there no longer, and the wall is capped with ugly cement. Everything neat and tidy, some might say; but not all, I think.

I hope the seeds from those lost valerians will seek other holes and crannies in the village, that they will beautify eventually other places, and that, upon reflection, there might be in someone's mind regret for what has rashly been done. For those valerians were beautiful, on the top of that wall.

This little area, the Millpool, was, in a way, a microcosm of the village itself, with its granite cottages — built, many of them, for less than a hundred pounds — its back cellars smelling of nets and ropes and tar, where expertly-placed granite steps led up to lofts supported by massive granite pillars.

Go down Duck Street, where once a river flowed, and you will find an opening on the left. It leads into a cluster of cellars and lofts and steps such as I have described. A lovely little patio in granite, and around you all the accommodation necessary for the activities of a fisherman long ago. Assuredly the baskets and nets and ropes have gone, but to one who crept in there inquisitively as a boy the memory and smell of it remains.

Some of the house fronts in the village were of dressed stone, of superior quality, reflecting perhaps the aspiration of fishermen who had had a succession of good seasons. The others were less pretentious, but with stones always skilfully placed.

I think there was at that time a feeling for stone, an ability to position it to the greatest advantage, an inherent artistry, which I feel, sadly, has almost been lost.

When stones fall from our Cornish hedges now, or are struck out by rash drivers, all too often they are replaced by shapeless masses of concrete; and even if stones are used in the replacement — the same stones perhaps — they bear no relation to their companions, in that the original pattern is rashly disturbed.

I shall never forget my cousin, a builder at Newlyn, pointing out to me the wall of an old store, and saying to me "Isn't that a lovely piece of walling?" I felt just like he did about that piece of wall, even before he told me to look up at it. He belonged, as his father did, and my father too, to a generation of builders in stone for whom a wall had to be not only strong, but a picture in itself, a pattern to be looked upon with pleasure.

There are exceptions to the criticisms I have made. I have seen building work in stone and repair work in hedges done well, and with feeling, in quite a few places of late, not only in private construction, but also in work ordered by the Penwith authorities. I see it in excellent walling opposite the Pirates' Hotel in Penzance, in the hedges towards the top of Paul Hill (now changed, unfortunately, to "Chywoone" Hill), and at Chyenall, to mention only a few places.

There is plenty of granite about still. Large boulders of it could well have been used to line the entrance to the new Telecom building in Mousehole Lane, which is astonishingly ugly with its concrete curbs and its offending wide, angular, or, shall I say, triangular, approach. I have felt sorry about that, and about any architect who could have devised it. And I think I am not alone in my feelings. It is a structure ill-conceived, quite out of keeping with the rest of the lane.

There **is** something in happy accord with the rest of the lane. Step down a little towards the village, just a few yards, in fact, and you will see — at the entrance to the old orchard, which, as I have said, is now a pleasant estate — a beautiful piece of hedging and terracing in granite, a speaking contrast and reproach to the distasteful construction in full view on the other side of the road.

I was there, only yesterday as I write. It was good, that piece of work, tastefully done, after my own heart. Hands from the past had told their secret to the young man I saw digging with a Cornish shovel in one of the terraces there. I was constrained to go up and speak to him, to congratulate him upon what had been done so lovingly and so well.

V
The Early Luggers. A Literary Contest.

There were many lime-washed cottages in Mousehole in the days I am speaking of. It was a traditional decoration, and must have helped a lot in the streets in the dark winter nights. The doors and windows were painted often a soft powder-blue, a colour which I think gave added beauty to these houses, blending in well with the white walls.

As we grew older in the Millpool we adventured deeper into the village, and came inevitably to the harbour and boats. We climbed the mooring chains to the decks of the luggers, climbed the masts, went down the companions to the curiously stuffy cabins, learnt to scull from the stern of the punts — in short, engaged in all the activities which led us to know the sea, and to be proficient later on in sailing our own craft. Of course, the luggers then were all sailing boats. Very few of them had motors of any type before about 1912. The only craft driven otherwise than by sail then were the large drifters from Lowestoft, fishing from Newlyn. They were steam-driven, magnificent boats, built for any weather. I have seen them come into harbour at Newlyn, after heavy weather, in a sorry state, with steel wheel-houses flattened and bulwarks wrecked. In 1926 there was a terrific gale, unusually fierce. Wives of the Lowestoft fishermen lodged at Newlyn had struggled, terrified, towards Mousehole, as far as Penlee, to scan the cauldron southwards from which any battered drifters might appear. They knew their own boats. They could distinguish them from afar. One can imagine their agony as they gazed, their fearful anticipation. One drifter, "The Faithful Friend" was overdue, and hope for her safety almost abandoned. I saw her come out of the haze, round the bend from Mousehole, as I stood on the north pier at Newlyn. She was safe, but severely battered. Her skipper, a middle-aged little chap, climbed the chain ladder to safety, raised his cap, and uttered two words only. They are vivid still in my mind: "Thank God!". "The Faithful Friend" had lived up to her name. If you wish to see her, in the condition in which she was that day, step into the Dolphin Inn at Newlyn. Her picture hangs upon the wall there, or did, when I last took a drink at that Inn.

We called those drifters "Yarkies" and "L.T's". They put out on Sundays — something approaching a crime to the strict Methodists of Mousehole and Newlyn at the time, and that was the cause of the serious riot just before the turn of the century, when infuriated local fishermen boarded the "Yarkies", and emptied their catch of mackerel into the harbour. I have recollections of my great uncle Tom boasting of certain Mousehole fishermen who, he said, "did a good job that day".

I shudder to think how much more violent the fishermen at St. Ives would have been in similar circumstances; for the religious prejudices were very strong indeed there, and have persisted almost to the present day. I believe it is still an adventure with uncertain consequences to put to sea on "the Blessed Sabbath" in that port.

I liked to see the "Yarkies", but it is of our beautiful luggers, their skilful intelligent crews, and the life surrounding them, that I wish to speak, and it will form, I hope, the bulk of my story.

The fishing boats at Mousehole, in the early years of last century, from about 1830 onwards, were very different from the splendid luggers, the "mackerel-drivers", as they were called, and the "pilchard-drivers", of 60 or 70 years later. The length of keel of these earlier boats did not exceed 25 feet. They were quite open to the weather, with only a small deck in the fore-part, then called a "cuddy". Lacking gangways or hatches, the only means of getting rid of any water shipped was by toiling hard at the pumps. Their rig was very different from the later luggers, too. They had three masts, and six sails — jib, foresail, mainsail, maintopsail, mizzen and mizzentopsail.

Most of the details I have given were supplied by Mr. Bernard Victor, of Wellington Place, Mousehole. They were contained in a contribution to the "Cornishman" or the "Cornish Telegraph", in about 1880. Mr. Victor says that at that time there were 60 boats engaged in the mackerel fishery; that they were 40 feet to 50 feet in length, and carried a crew of seven hands as against the six hands of the earlier boats. He gives a list of Mousehole boats on the mackerel fishery, and their owners, in the early part of last century, about 1830, which might be of interest to some families in the village today. I will include them in my account:

George (Richard Harvey & J. Trewavas)
Resolution (John Pezzack)
Unity (Thomas Pentreath & John Bodinnar)
Mars (John Harvey & Pezzack)
Betsy (Alexander Harvey)
Three Brothers (John Johns & J. Pentreath)
Brothers (Thomas Mann)
Two Brothers (James Pentreath)
Three Brothers (Richard Ladner)
Flora (John James Wright)
Gregor (John Wright)
Return (Thomas Wallis)
May Flower (Richard Yeoman)
Mary (Richard Angwin)
Mary Ann (Hugh Jacka & J. Madron)
Friendship (Charles Harvey & Michael Wright)

Friends (Thomas Keigwin & Francis Richards)
John and Jane (John Gruzelier & John Badcock)
Barbadoes (Edward Quick & Margaret Matthews)
Union (Richard Mann)
Industry (William Harvey)
Dashwood (John Blewett)
Endeavour (John Harvey & John C. Wright)
Amicable (John Wright & William Rearden)
Elizabeth (Peter Downing)
Bounty (John Pender & J. Wright)
Hope (Richard Pentreath)
Enterprise (Joseph Humphrys)

Twenty-eight in all.

Mr. Bernard Victor seems to have been a very scholarly man, with considerable knowledge of the Old Cornish Language and the many activities of his native village. He contributed articles to the local papers of the day, especially "The Cornishman", "The Cornish Telegraph"; even "The Tidings" of that time. His name can be coupled with that of another erudite gentleman, Mr. F.W. Pentreath, also of Mousehole, for both took part in an interesting competition. At a celebration of the Centenary of the death of Dolly Pentreath — reputedly the last person to converse in the Cornish Language — at Paul, in 1877, it was decided, largely by the efforts and enthusiasm of the Rev. Lach-Szyrma, Vicar of St. Peter's, Newlyn, himself a notable student of the Celtic Language, and author of a "History of Penzance and Land's End", that a prize should be offered for an essay on "The Ancient Cornish Language". Accordingly, essays were written by the two gentlemen I have mentioned, and submitted for consideration to Professor John Rhys, M.A., Professor of Celtic at Oxford University, and Mr. J. Henry Jenner, of the British Museum.

The judges were ultimately in agreement, and decided that, the essays being of equal merit, the prize should be divided equally between the contestants. Each essay contained a glossary of Old Cornish words. Professor Rhys was of the opinion that Mr. Victor's glossary was fuller than Mr. Pentreath's, adding that both men had been guilty of including in their lists of Cornish words several which, in his opinion, had been borrowed from English. An interesting comment from Mr. Jenner was that whilst admiring what he called the "Celtic eloquence" of Mr. Victor's composition, he preferred "the more scientific collection of dry facts" in that of Mr. Pentreath.

The prizes were duly presented, in 1879, to the two Mousehole gentlemen, in St. Peter's schoolroom at Newlyn, by the vicar, who was thanked sincerely by both contestants.

I must mention here that a glossary of Old Cornish words and meanings had been sent, much earlier than those of the two contestants, to the British Museum by a Mousehole man, Jacob George, grandfather to Nettie Mann Pender, in the year 1868. It was entitled "Memorandum of Old Cornish words still current in Mousehole and Newlyn".

From the glossary of Cornish words included in the two essays I give here a list of 30, quite a number of which can be heard spoken today, and all of which were quite familiar to me as a boy:

Bal: a mine.
Beety: to mend nets.
Bussa: a large earthenware pot.
Clomb: earthenware.
Cowleck: a greedy person.
Creature: missel-thrush.
Crowst: refreshment for labourers in the fields.
Drethan: a stretch of sand under the water.
Fuggan: an unleavened cake.
Garm: a cry of anguish or alarm.
Hilla: nightmare.
Jowdy: to walk in the sea with boots and stockings on.
Kiskey: a rotten stick or stalk.
Lagging: walking in shallow water with bare feet (children).
Leary: faint with hunger.
Lewth: shelter from the weather.
Meryan: an ant.
Minch: to play truant at school.
Mor: a thin root, of a tree, etc.
Pelf: small particles of wool, etc., on one's clothes.
Planchen: wooden floor
Quilken: a young frog
Scat: to hit, break to pieces.
Scaw (pronounced "scao"): elder.
Stank: to tread on.
Tic: feather mattress.
Totling: senile, foolish.
Towser: apron of coarse cloth worn by wives of fishermen.
Zad: the letter Z.
Zawn: a cave, cavern.

VI
Hevva!

Fishing in Cornwall took a considerable step forward in the eighteenth century, during the course of which there were tremendous shoals of pilchards coming from farther north into our warmer waters. They came in the summer time, from July onwards.

In the ensuing century, whilst the luggers, gradually improving in size and efficiency, shot their nets for herring and mackerel, and pilchards too, in the appropriate seasons, even going as far as Ireland, the major industry by far in Cornwall was the inshore seine-fishing. This was, of course, an industry, not continuous, dependent on chance, but enormous quantities of pilchards were landed at times to supplement the catches of the drifters at sea, and give employment to a great number of the village folk at Mousehole, St. Ives, and the other fishing villages in Cornwall. According to the writer I have quoted previously there were nearly 3,000 persons employed on the seine boats in 1827 and at least 6,000 indirectly engaged ashore.

The seine, or "sean", to give it its original name, was a composite unit comprising two nets, the smaller of which was called the "tuck-net", and three or four accompanying boats. I shall here describe only one seine putting to sea. There were, in fact, a large number of seines always ready for putting out, especially at St. Ives, where, in 1930, there were upwards of 100. So many, that half that number were usually sufficient to deal with heavy shoals of pilchards there, and an agreement was made whereby the others stayed ashore. The agreement was not always honoured when times had been bad and unemployment rife. All the seines would then put to sea.

What was it like, this seine-fishing? Well, there would be watchers, "huers" as they were called, ashore, at strategic points on the cliff tops. They would be looking for the curious agitation of the waters offshore, the shadowy patches, which indicated to their experienced eyes shoals of pilchards — or "schools', as we called them. The cry of "Hevva! Hevva!" repeated time and time again, would rouse the whole startled and expectant village, and men would rush to man the seine-boats.

These boats were built for the work they were now setting out to accomplish. They would be, I should say, about 30 or 40 feet long, a sort of long-boat or gig, with several pairs of oars, originally owned by some well-to-do and adventurous person ashore, who paid the fishermen for their work.

The boats would proceed rapidly to sea, the men aboard observing carefully the "huer" upon the cliff top, who would direct them by his motions — manipulating perhaps a couple of so-called "bushes" in his hands — to the school of fish. With more precise directions then from the huer, with his tin trumpet, the fishermen, with remarkable celerity and skill, would cast their net, rowing at full speed, frantically, in the process, in order to encircle the school of pilchards. That operation completed, they would keep thrashing the water with their oars in order to prevent the escape over the top of the net of the luckless prey. The ends of the net would then be drawn together, and the whole struggling mass of pilchards trapped.The net, supported by corks and held rigid with lead sinkers, would reach the bottom and prevent escape in that direction. The tuck-net would be lowered into the seething mass, and, when full, drawn to the side of the waiting boats. The pilchards would be dipped up in baskets and transferred laboriously into the waiting craft before being taken ashore to the cellars.

In those circles of tumult, those cauldrons, the whole of the "seines" having been shot, there might be millions of fish. In former days, if the operation was carried out closer to the land, the trawl-net might have been drawn shorewards, and the fish removed with the help of the same tuck-net. The operation would take quite a time.

"Tucking a School of Pilchards", by Percy Craft

Ashore, the fishermen and their wives would be working hard in their cellars "bulking" the pilchards; that is, arranging them in flat layers, tier upon tier, and adding coarse salt generously to each layer as they built them up for curing against some convenient wall. It was a skilful, and laborious, proceeding, improved upon vastly later and rendered quite unnecessary (though depriving many people of employment) when curing in tanks was introduced. These tanks, as I remember them, were usually about a nine or ten foot cube in size, and would hold close on 100,000 pilchards.

I am leaping forward in time, and must eventually go back and try to give an account of the early mackerel and herring fishery. But it will be easier for me here to complete my picture of the pilchard industry, more especially as I knew it in the early years of this century.

In the new large cellars the fish were shovelled into the tanks — a layer of pilchards, a layer of coarse salt, another layer with coarse salt, and so on until the tank was full. After several weeks a lot of brine would have developed, and the fish would be ready to be taken out.

The salt employed in this operation, latterly, was a special product brought from the Bay of Setubal, in Portugal, in vessels which berthed in the harbour at Mousehole and the other ports. The coming of any large vessel was quite an event in our village.

A man with a basket and top boots — leather at the time, as all the fishermen's boots at that time were — would go into the tank, supported at first by floating planks, dip his basket into the mass of fish, and hand it up full to the waiting arms above. As the tanks were emptied, the fish would be placed in barrels by fisher-wives expert in the task. They wore "towsers", rough aprons, as they placed the fish, heads outwards, in a magnificently-executed circle, row upon row. The smell in the cellar was strong, of fish and oil and brine, warm, pervading, unforgettable.

The barrels were about two feet six high and fifteen inches in diameter — a rough estimate which I hope is correct enough. When full, pressure was put upon the fish from above, and increased at intervals until they had been flattened, the valuable pilchard oil extracted, and the barrels sealed ready for transport to the traditional Italian markets. I think Genoa was the principal market, but the fish went also to Leghorn, Naples, Venice and Trieste.

I have spoken mainly so far of the seining industry, but it must not be forgotten that the luggers, the drifters, the "pilchard-drivers", casting their nets in deeper waters, had long been a continuous and more dependable source of pilchards than the seine-boats, operating as the latter did only when large shoals visited our coasts. There was at times ill feeling between the pilchard-drivers and the seiners, the latter complaining that the offshore boats, shooting a wall of nets miles long, were apt to arrest the progress of the shoals into shallow water and change their direction.

The pilchard-drivers sent their catches to the same Italian ports that I have mentioned. Their success varied, and there was great poverty at times in the villages, not only because of the lack of pilchards, but because of the scarcity of mackerel and herring too. Many of our fishermen had to go into the Navy, the Merchant Service and Yachting, where their acquired skill was valued enormously. Others, for whom there was no prospect in the fishing, strove hard to find employment elsewhere. Two elderly sisters of my acquaintance in the village, speaking of the hard times when they were young, told me that their father, having obtained temporary work at the tin mines, would set out at four o'clock of a Monday morning to face a near ten-mile walk, over rough roads, to St. Just. Home on Wednesday, for a short time, he would set out again the next morning to complete the week's arduous task.

They well remember him also, with others, trudging to St. Ives, even, eleven miles away, in the hope of finding a berth in one of the luggers there. It was a struggle indeed, in those days.

Some fishermen were accused at times of laziness, of lacking the initiative to seek alternative employment. It must be remembered that the sea was their life, a domain exclusively their own, and hard it was, indeed, for them to envisage any other. They bore hard times with great courage.

The year 1907, says Mr. Hamilton Jenkin, "witnessed practically the last of the big seine catches — 24 millions of fish having been netted that year in St. Ives' Bay."

Big catches did occur at times later than the year just mentioned. I remember my father receiving, more than once, an urgent message: "Seine-shot at Sennen!" and proceeding on his bike at once to cover the ten miles to Sennen early enough to make his bid for the catches. Big schools of pilchards were often seen at Sennen Cove.

The Italian merchants were tricky to deal with at times, and, of course, there were difficulties of language. At times the fish arriving in their ports might be declared of inferior quality — the truth of which could not easily be determined. Upon the whole, however, the trade was satisfactory, though it had been in the farther past interrupted by conflicts such as the Napoleonic Wars, which had necessitated the search for new markets.

I have pleasant memories of meeting two Italian merchants, to whom my father sent pilchards, at Genoa — Pittaluga and Marabotti — who, one after the other, treated myself and my two brothers, on our way to Egypt, to enormous and expensive meals. I wasn't too well at the time, and quite unable to get through all the courses that Pittaluga had ordered. In fact, the first course, ample and delicious, a sort of spaghetti served with meat, was quite enough for me. My brothers proceeded, after not a long break, to Marabotti's, where, they said, the meal they encountered was even more ample and rich than the one which Pittaluga had provided. The Italians do seem to eat heavily. I had had, perforce, to decline the invitation to Marabotti's.

It might interest my readers to know that the price of pilchards at Mousehole — say a little before 1920 — was about 25 shillings a thousand, and sometimes as low as 15 shillings a thousand; less than the price of a fair-sized pollack today. Indeed, I am quite sure, having been allowed to peruse the remarkably interesting records of my uncle Herbert, that at times the price was well below ten shillings a thousand.

I made some reference a little way back to the bad times of the pilchard industry and the poverty that existed in many villages, and I must not conclude my account of that industry without telling a little more of the sad distress of those times.

During the long struggle with Napoleon, when there was no longer access to the European countries, new markets had somehow to be found, and during the search there was great poverty almost everywhere, especially in the Isles of Scilly, in the long periods when the pilchard shoals seemed to disappear altogether, to deprive the families of what had become their staple food.

It is difficult to imagine the distress of those years, augmented as it was by the suppression of smuggling, and, in Scilly, by the frequent failure of the potato crop. The situation on the Islands and on the mainland was worse in the early years of last century, before the repeal of the hated Salt Tax in about 1830, salt being essential for the curing of the pilchards.

The authorities were often kindly disposed at times when people depending on fish had no money to purchase the necessary salt. In 1812, for example, the Bishop of Exeter became aware of great need in Scilly, and ordered salt to be sent from Penzance and sold to the poor there free of duty. Private individuals, too, were compassionate. In 1811 a Mr. Blewett, of Marazion, supplied the poor with as much salt as was necessary to cure large quantities of pilchards which he had distributed at the low price of one shilling per hundred. Indeed, to those unable to afford even that, he gave both fish and salt free.

The salt came principally from Cheshire, and was called Pit Salt. It was sometimes drastically reduced in price — in 1822 from 15/- to 2/- a bushel — which price was still too dear for many poor people. The salt imported from France — the trade was resumed after 1815 — tended to rise heavily in price. It was much more suitable for the export pilchards than the Pit Salt, for the latter tended to give them an unacceptable rusty colour.

In the search for new markets there was one conspicuous success. Cured pilchards were sent to the West Indies, to the plantation owners, who supplied them to their negro slaves as food. It is interesting also to record that many well-to-do farmers provided their own seines and bought pilchards from the fishermen to spread as valuable manure on their land.

Lack of markets for fish and the high price of salt were not the only troubles the fishers had to face. They were liable to the payment of tithes, and this was hotly resented. The Church was in the habit of leasing out the collection of tithes — which is not surprising when one considers the hazardous nature of the operation in times of distress. Resentment flared in Mousehole and Newlyn when the lessees had the temerity to increase these tithes, in 1830, to £6 per boat. A solicitor who came to demand payment was very roughly handled, and a bailiff who came later to serve writs was fortunate to escape alive. The Newlyn women tore the clothes from his body. It had been a question of paying tithes or going short of bread.

Remarkably generous help of a practical nature was given to the people of the Isles of Scilly in the difficult periods of which I have written, when there was no prospect for them in the pilchard and mackerel fisheries, by a Society called the "Industrious Society". They obtained sufficient money by subscription to establish shore industries on the Islands. They sent a spinning-wheel; and later, under their auspices, a group of girls from Mousehole and Newlyn were sent to instruct in the making of stockings, frocks, gloves, straw hats and other articles which were later brought to Penzance and sold at a depot there.

VII
The Mackerel-Drivers. Fitting Out.

The pilchard fishery, especially the seining, of which, from details I have read, and from my own memory, I have tried to give a reasonable account, was preceded by the mackerel fishery. This occurred during the Spring months, up to the beginning of June, and also, earlier on, in the late Autumn, from September onwards to December.

I think, before I attempt any account of that fishing, however, I must describe the beautiful "mackerel-drivers" — as we called them — the boats which had developed during the nineteenth century from the open-decked craft I have spoken of to the swift, graceful boats of the latter years of that century, and of which the "pilchard-drivers" were a smaller model.

They were sailing craft, and this book is my dream of them. I have not the knowledge to go beyond the time when they filled the harbour at Mousehole. They were lugger-rigged, that is to say with square sails hung from a yard fastened obliquely to the mast. Lug sails were the common rig for centuries in this country up to the first half of the last century, and, indeed, had always been the traditional rig of the fishing-boats in most of the countries of Northern Europe.

It was a practical rig in a way, and beautiful to look upon when the sails were full, but defective, perhaps, in one respect. In tacking, or putting the boat about, the sail had to be lowered, and the heavy yard transferred to the other side of the mast. This was an operation requiring skill and speed, and hazardous indeed in heavy weather, all the more so as the ballast, consisting early of heavy stones and later of half-hundred-weights, had to be shifted speedily at the same time. It was probably for this reason that the East Country trawlers and drifters changed slowly from lugger rig to what was termed "ketch rig", though the Lowestoft fishermen continued to call their drifters "luggers", wrongly. Their trawlers were known as "smacks", a term loosely used, but signifying generally a ketch-rigged boat. These trawlers and drifters came to our own shores here in Mount's Bay. I believe the trawlers kept the boom on their mainsails. The drifters, still ketch-rigged, but with loose-footed mainsails, giving greater room for manoeuvre amidships, were known to our fishermen as "dandies".

Brixham trawlers came to our Bay too. Their rig resembled that of the East Country boats, but they had square sterns instead of the rounded or elliptical sterns of the former. These trawlers and drifters, whether from Lowestoft or Brixham, were admired immensely by our fishermen.

The Scottish fishermen stuck to their lugger rig for a long time, almost up to the period when steam was introduced.

Our own mackerel and herring-drivers, or luggers, were about 50 feet long, with a beam of perhaps 15 feet.

Most of them, including the smaller pilchard-boats, were built at Porthleven, across the bay from Mousehole; others at Newlyn, or St. Ives, or Penzance. They sat like ducks upon the water. To see them heeling over in a breeze, with full sails, especially at Regatta times in the Bay, was a pleasurable sight indeed. I have often wondered about their graceful design, and where it originated. They were framed in oak, with pitch-pine masts and planking, and top-rails mostly of elm. Their sterns drew to a point like their bows, but a few had square sterns, such as the "Edgar", P.Z. 131, and the "Hopeful", P.Z. 634. I remember that some of the luggers, early on, had their tallest masts aft, and carried topsails, called locally "mizzen-poles", above their mizzens.

Porthleven seems to have had important boat-building yards for a very long time. As I have said, most of our sailing luggers were built there, and even some trawlers and drifters from Yarmouth and Lowestoft.

I have before me, as I write, a picture, taken from the Western Morning News of October 10/1980, of "Chamois", L.T. 3 — "running for Penzance under storm canvas". It was taken in 1884 by Gibson, of Penzance — locally renowned for his magnificent pictures of scenes, and wrecks especially, in West Cornwall. The "Chamois" seemed to me at first like one of our own luggers, but my friend David, looking at her with a sailor's eye, had no doubt that she was an East Country boat, ketch-rigged. It did seem to me, looking at her from stem to stern, end-on, as it were, her rig ragged and close-hauled, that her hull especially resembled that of our own boats. Perhaps she was built at Porthleven.

The firm of Kitto, at Porthleven, will be well-known to our fishermen, as also will Peake's of Newlyn, Triggs of Newlyn, and Trevorrow of St. Ives. When I was a boy some boats were built at Mousehole, on the far strand, by the family Williams, living on the bank above the North Pier, in the last house before the path went down to the beach where ladies put their washing out to dry. The "Edgar", owned by Percy Laity, was built there, and another boat called the "Coronation". I can well remember the shaping of the "Edgar", and the skilful work of the adze upon her hull; the caulking, too. The adze seemed to me a remarkably well-shaped tool for the job it had to do.

I think I might take the beautiful lugger, the "Nellie Jane", P.Z. 130, owned by the Worth family, of Mousehole, as representative of the mackerel-drivers; and perhaps the "Ellen", P.Z. 306, owned by Stanley Drew, as representative of the equally beautiful pilchard-drivers.

The "Nellie" was built at Porthleven, and the "Ellen" at Trevorrow's, St Ives. The "Ellen" was graceful and swift. Her contests with the "Mary", owned, I think, by Percy Laity, were notable. Johnnie Drew, engineer on the Mousehole lifeboats for many years, and son to Stanley Drew, told me that the "Mary" defeated the "Ellen" only once in regattas. I wonder if the "Ellen" made a poor tack on that luckless regatta day, or whether Johnnie, rightly proud of that pilchard-driver, exaggerated just a little.

In mentioning these two boats I am in no way forgetting others that approached their excellence in both appearance and performance. Some I shall be pleased to speak of again.

Sid Pender told me that the luggers at Mevagissey were smaller than the Mount's Bay boats. He seemed to think that the latter were copied by the fishermen of the Isle of Man. There were slight differences in the design of the luggers, varying from place to place. Any improvements made were the result of careful experiment and knowledgeable seamanship.

The nets for the pilchard, herring and mackerel fisheries were purchased mainly from Gale & Sons, of Bridport in Dorset; also from Tucker & Gundry. They varied in size of mesh, of course, the pilchard nets having 36 to 38 meshes to the yard, the herring nets 30 to 32 to the yard, and the mackerel nets 25 to 26. In early days the fisherwomen frequently "breeded" their own nets.

The ropes could be obtained locally at the Yarmouth Stores opposite the Fish Market in Newlyn, and the sails from sailmaker Harris in his loft above the barking-house in Mousehole, or from Peter Hosking in his loft on the slip leading down to the south pier in Newlyn. I can well remember, as a boy, climbing the stairs to the wondrous place where sailmaker Harris worked.

All these — nets, sails and ropes would be preserved by immersion in vats containing catechu, or "cutch" as we always called it. Cutch came from Burma. It was a dark extract from the bark of several Indian plants of the same family as acacia or betel-nut, and rich in tannin. It gave to the sails of the luggers their delightful and distinctive shade of brown.

My uncle had what we termed a "bark-house" at the back of the "Cliff" at Mousehole. It was a sort of cellar with three coal-fired furnaces lined with iron or copper and surrounded by brick. The cutch was tipped into boiling water in these furnaces, and when dissolved tapped off into vats. Nets from the lofts above — the lofts having now been turned into flats — were payed out through trap-hatches straight down into these vats. Other nets, ropes and sails would be brought into the cellar by horse and cart, or in wheel-barrows, and immersed in a similar manner. The nets would be pulled out of the vats over a roller, piled high, and drained a little before being taken down to the harbour rails to dry, and eventually to the waiting boats.

My uncle, and doubtless other traders from Mevagissey and Looe, obtained this cutch from George Kenyon, Ltd., at Liverpool, the importers. It was sent by rail to Penzance, and thence by horse and cart to Mousehole. It was packed in flattish, substantial boxes, constructed of a sort of bastard mahogany, and in appearance resembled brown pieces of solid glue. These boxes were a great temptation to us as boys. They were kept in one of the lofts above the barking-house, and we crept there at times to get hold of an empty, or nearly empty, box, for they made excellent go-carts, wheels of which, in those days, were the sheaves of disused blocks from the luggers. I felt pleased when my cousin Vaughan told me that he still possessed two of his father's cutch-boxes. I could see that he was proud of those boxes, and of the work in which his father had been engaged; and my mind went back, with his, to that small loft where the cutch was stored.

I am not a fisherman, and it is therefore not easy for me to give an accurate account of the complicated process of removing nets from the luggers and fitting them out anew, according to the seasons. From the good help I have received, however, from my fisher friends, and from my own recollections, I can, I hope, give a fair picture. And if some fisherman tells me — and he will have to be old, like me — that I have been wrong in certain details, I shall bow to his superior knowledge.

At the change of season the nets would be taken out to dry, and would be spread wherever there was room for that purpose — over ropes slung between the masts, over the Cliff rails, across spars leading down from the Cliff to what we called the "por"; and, indeed, if space were unavailable elsewhere, taken in wagons up Raginnis Hill to the fields as far as Love Lane, and there spread out to dry. When I think of that, I think often, too, that the weather must really have been finer in those days than it is now.

When dry, the nets would be gathered and stored in the various lofts in the village. Of course, there were scores of lofts. The one above my uncle's bark-house was two-storeyed, capacious, and contained bundle after bundle of dried nets. And amid the good smell of those nets could be seen, often, the village women busy at "beeting", or mending, the nets. When any particular nets were required again, at the change of seasons, they would be taken from the lofts, treated with the preservative I have described, and taken, sometimes dripping, in barrows, sometimes slung over the shoulders of some sturdy fisher, to the waiting luggers.

Between seasons, prior to fitting out for a new fishing-ground, the fishermen would engage in a process of decoration of their luggers called "paying-up". It was a curious expression, and I have often wondered where it came from. In my study of Old French, a long time ago, I came across a verb — now disused, I think — written "peier", which meant "to pitch" or "decorate". There are innumerable words and names of French origin in our village, and it is possible that "paying-up" has a French origin.

There came first, in this work of refurbishing, the tarring of the whole hull of the luggers. The crews employed stubby brushes with long handles for this, standing on the harbour floor, reaching upwards after dipping their brushes in the pots of tar. It was rather a messy business, and the fishermen were not too concerned at getting their hands full of tar. The bottoms were tarred too, but later, I think, a special preservative against decay and marine growth was used for that, whilst the tarring gave place to painting.

The painting-in of the boats' numbers was often a challenge for someone not necessarily a fisherman. I remember well one of my older brothers being very keen on that work, and I can see him now painting carefully the number of the pilchard-driver "Nonpareil", which we called "Numparell". I can remember most of the boats' numbers in our harbour, and her number was P.Z. 166.

The painting of the "stroke" — the thin decorative line running from stem to stern, just under the gunwale — needed particular care. A blue stroke indicated a death, and a white stroke was for mourning.

Pictures of the luggers I have described can be seen in shops and studios all over Cornwall. Go down the steps into Mr. Huband's studio, opposite the Mill House in Mousehole, and you will see — interspersed with quaint pictures of the village itself long ago — faithful paintings of the old luggers. They have captured the imagination and love of this artist, as they have, similarly, of the painter up the steps, just above, Mr. Hallard.

Step into the King's Arms — and you can, without a tremor now, for when I was a boy a man would hesitate to cross that threshold, for fear of being dubbed a drunkard, and never a woman would be seen — walk along its ancient granite floors to the quiet lounge beyond, and you will see upon the wall there a picture of some luggers quietly at anchor in the harbour. I can remember one of them myself, as I look upon it — the "Activity", P.Z. 573. The luggers you look at will **really** be quietly at anchor, too, for, happily, the noise of modern music is absent from that lovely old-fashioned Inn, except at rare moments.

If you wish to see the best picture of all, of the luggers, go through the swing doors of Barclay's Bank, at Penzance, and upon the wall there, on the left of the rather beautiful lamps, you will see the pride of that interior — a painting of Mousehole harbour, looked at from the Wharf, with the larger luggers in startling array, and the sun gloriously bright upon the northern pier. The boats are **really** boats, but not photographic. There is no travesty of the truth. It is a study of love.

The painter was Stanhope Forbes. I think, as he looked upon those luggers, straining a little at their moorings, that he was conscious of the strong pulse of the village life.

The Luggers. Picture by Stanhope Forbes

VIII
The Mackerel Fishery

The port was busy during early March. The nets that were stored in the lofts had been immersed in the preserving vats, dried as far as possible, taken, still dripping at times, on flat barrows, on the shoulders of fishermen, to the waiting, impatient luggers. The village was expectant, astir. The mackerel season had begun.

The proud luggers in the harbour cast their chains, marked their positions with cork buoys, and eased out from their moorings towards the gaps. Unhurriedly, skilfully, in the limited space available. They would soon hoist their sails and proceed to the fishing-grounds.

It was not easy at times, when the surge was strong, for the crews to negotiate the gaps and reach the open. Various methods of warping-out were employed, some described to me by my fishermen friends. I have myself seen some of them in operation. I think the most successful method was for the fishermen to pull upon a strong rope attached to their boat's anchor that had been dropped well out towards the Island. I believe there was an iron ring on the island used for this warping-out at times, but the operation was not always successful because of the chafing of the rope against the sharp rocks.

Mackerel-fishing had for centuries been an important industry in Cornwall, carried on especially by the Mount's Bay and St. Ives luggers. The main season, as I have indicated above, lasted from March to the beginning of the pilchard season in July; but some boats fished also in the Autumn.

One might naturally wonder how, before the railway came to Penzance in 1859, the landings of mackerel, large at times, were disposed of. Well, they were, of course, sold locally, either transported by horse and cart through the villages and countryside, or carried, laboriously, by the fisherwives themselves in a big ingeniously-constructed basket strapped behind their shoulders. The fisherwives were not always young, indeed quite elderly at times. There is no lack of paintings and prints to illustrate this quaint old trade.

It was customary at St. Ives, in the early part of last century, for mackerel to be taken in vessels to Bristol, and from there to the London market in carts or vans. The journey to Billingsgate would take up to three or four days. It is possible that a similar practice obtained from the harbours at Mousehole and Newlyn, with Plymouth perhaps as the first objective, but I cannot be sure of that. In any case, it was necessary for the transport to London to be as swift as possible, for the mackerel is a fish that does not keep fresh for long.

At Mousehole, if the tide was low, the luggers returning with their catches would anchor "'tween isle and shore", and waiting jolly-boats, captained usually by boys, called "yawlers", would take the fish and men ashore. The same process obtained at Newlyn, where a much larger fleet than at Mousehole had to moor permanently offshore, and depend upon their own yawlers to land the catch and the men.

All this was changed, dramatically, as soon the first engine puffed into the new station at Penzance, in 1859. There was now access for the fishers to the vast market of London, and Newlyn became a more important base than ever. Competition was keen to land catches for the early trains, and faster and larger boats had to be built. And so, in the latter part of last century, the luggers achieved their final glory.

The yawlers were now engaged in a different and more exciting operation. They would put out in the track of the returning luggers off Mousehole, and, skilfully adopting a parallel course, cast the ropes they carried accurately, at a given moment, to make contact and be drawn speedily, in a glorious ride, bows uplifted, towards Newlyn, where they would take the fish and crews ashore.

I was never a yawler. But I would have taken great joy in that sweeping voyage. Those mackerel-drivers were fast sailers, and the boys in those jolly-boats, especially if the wind was fresh and behind them, would be well paid for the extraordinary skill they had shown at the outset in making contact with the luggers. In any case, the various manoeuvres in which they had constantly to engage was a valuable apprenticeship indeed to the varied professions they would adopt in later years.

The completion of the large harbour at Newlyn in 1886 was the cause of further dramatic changes in the Mount's Bay mackerel fishery. Up to that point our luggers had been free of serious rivals, for only a few of the East Country sailing trawlers and drifters had frequented our waters. It is not surprising, therefore, that their numbers increased rapidly when they were able to enter a safe port and land their catches on the Newlyn quays. It was unfortunate for our fishermen, for they could scarcely compete against the massive instrusion. The situation became even more desperate for them when, a few years before the end of last century, the East Coast drifters installed steam engines and became the "yarkies" I have already described, which fished on the Sabbath and incurred the wrath of our own fishermen.

It is probable that the intrusion of so many East Country drifters was the cause of a gradual decline in the local mackerel fishery from that time. It continued, however, after the turn of the century. Some of the boats, fishing deep beyond Scilly, carried on as usual, staying afloat for days on end, carrying ice, and, if head winds prevented their return to harbour, would sail to some Irish port such as Kinsale, sell their catch there, and operate from there for a time. Some boats would fish close off Scilly and land their catches there. Others would still fish closer to home waters, bring their fish to Mousehole, thus avoiding the trip to Newlyn, and get them transported to the new fishmarket there by horse and cart.

The mackerel fishery was at times fraught with danger. Sudden gales would spring up, and quick decisions had to be made. The boats would put into Scilly for shelter if possible. In the increasing tempest the shawled and white-faced women of the village would gather in the shops, in Susan Mary's shop perhaps, seeking a certain consolation in numbers, waiting for the message that would calm their fears — the message that such-and-such a boat was safe in Scilly. I have a vivid memory of the anxious faces of those days.

As the mackerel fishery gradually declined, and the schools of fish became scarcer, new methods of fishing had to be found, such as long-lining, and a different type of engine-driven craft constructed. But of these I cannot speak, lacking the necessary knowledge, and concerned as I am, mainly, with the old sailing-boats. The herring fishery, however, persisted for quite a time, gaining a certain impetus from the slowing down of its companion industry.

It is to that herring fishery that I must now return. First of all, however, it is fitting for me to mention that at the end of the mackerel season, and during the pilchard season in July and August, some of the bigger luggers laid up for a while before fitting out again for the Plymouth herring fishery, whilst others, in company with somewhat smaller boats which we called "half-and-halfers" went "haking" or "pollacking", with single lines, and sometimes with considerable success. The hakes were hung upon the outside walls of the cottages, in the sun, to dry, and as boys we picked pieces of them to eat as we ran about the village. Hake, that prime fish, so dear today, was a great stand-by when times were bad in the villages of Mousehole, Newlyn and St. Ives.

At the same period, in July and August, several of the bigger luggers sailed to Ireland instead of laying up, to take part in the summer herring fishery, which was carried on at the same time in the North Sea. The Irish herring were regarded by our fishermen as something special.

IX
The Herring Fishery. Life at the Barbican.

According to the important book by Carew, "Survey of Cornwall", written in 1602, the herring fishery in Cornwall and Devon was mainly at first a coastal trade. It is astonishing, however, to learn that in that same century some fishermen had ventured much further afield, first to Ireland, and later even to the North Sea and Scotland.

I would like to have some light shed upon those voyages of long ago, those courageous undertakings; some detailed record of the incredible risks taken by men whose reward was at times very small indeed. We can imagine the discomfort in the small undecked craft, the cramped conditions, the storms encountered, the hazardous runs for shelter, the uncertainties of the market ashore, the silent, and uttered, prayer, as the first net was cast, the elation when they struck the herring shoals; and, finally, we can see the eyes cast towards home, the far-distant happy haven. It has been the theme for many a feeling artist, and understandably so: the staunch partner at home, patiently beautiful at morning-tide, sitting at her table, waiting. It was not often, happily, a "Hopeless Dawn". An unexpected clamour in the port, a step upon the stair from the cellar below, a joyous light in her eyes, and for her the long, loyal vigil would be over.

In the seventeenth and eighteenth centuries the herring fishery in Cornwall and Devon continued to be mainly a coastal trade except for the adventurous journeys to Ireland and further afield that I have already mentioned. The herring shoals around the Cornish coasts were plentiful at times, but there were occasions when they seemed to disappear altogether. And there was no great change in this respect in the last century, when the boats were becoming bigger and more efficient. It was observed by the "West Briton", in 1839, that in that year the season in Ireland proved to be a complete failure. Failures such as this were a serious matter for the local population, and many families suffered great hardship. I have an interesting note in my Uncle Herbert's diary relating that, in 1896, "owing to the failure of the North Sea herring fishery, our fishing-boats went to Skibbereen (S. Ireland) for the mackerel fishing."

Later on in the century, when the luggers had achieved their final glory, and up to, perhaps, the early years of the present century, when the first motor was installed in the "Edgar", the offshore and Irish herring fisheries continued, but gradually became less important as the North Sea — before the discovery of the Bigberry Bay shoals at Plymouth — became a more easily attainable and profitable fishing ground. The big, proud luggers would fit out and follow the same route as the adventurous fishermen of old, though much freer from the hazards encountered then. Some would go to Howth, north of Dublin, thence to the Isle of Man and Scotland, through the Caledonian Canal, drawn by horses, and down the East Coast to Sunderland, Hartlepool, Whitby, Scarborough, Yarmouth, Lowestoft. Following the shoals, the insistent shoals seeking always warmer shores.

The journey was sometimes made in reverse, the luggers sailing straight to the North Sea and ending their long search in Ireland again, at Howth, or Kinsale, or Ardglass.

The homecoming of the boats was a joyous affair, and presents would be brought. There were Paisley shawls from Scotland, jet jewellery from Whitby, Scarborough rock for the children, and for the boys a pocket knife from Ireland, much prized, of fine steel, known as a "barber". I cannot forget the shawled fisherwomen in Susan Mary's shop, a common sight in those days.

I think our fishermen rather enjoyed their stay in Ireland; more so, perhaps, than in any of the North Sea ports, for I often heard them speak happily of their adventures there when I was a boy. I must not forget to relate, however, that my fisherman friend Jack Pender, at the age of 13, in 1903, shipped with skipper George Dennis in the new sailing-lugger "Edgar", and went to Scarborough for the summer herring fishery, as cook. He was delighted with Scarborough. "A lovely place to go ashore in weekends," he said, "with plenty of ice cream and amusements." A pleasing boy's reaction, indeed.

I have related how our fishermen seemed to find themselves at home in Ireland. It had something to do, maybe, with similarity of race and way of life. But there were brawls at times, especially when some of our men, relishing perhaps for a moment emancipation from the strict rules at home, would become more vocal than usual at Mother Rickard's or Findlater's or Cassidy's, hostelries at Howth. In my great-uncle's stories there were vague suggestions of sudden conflict, of "bars having been cleared!" Of course, there were, in any case, very few of our fishermen who would enter a public house. Those who did would probably be quite as tough as their Irish opponents, well able to play their part. But we must forget these rare encounters.

With the fortunate, and fortuitous, discovery of the plentiful fishing grounds off Plymouth, in Bigberry Bay, our sailing-luggers discontinued their journeys to the North Sea in search of herring. Three luggers — the "Children's Friend", P.Z. 619, the "Emblem", P.Z. 575, and the "Nellie Jane", P.Z. 130, did make the trip as late as 1909, accomplishing the journey to Scarborough in fast time, in spite of adverse weather conditions, making the run in seventy hours.

But Plymouth was now our chief fishing base for herring. In 1907, says Sid Pender, there were 30 boats from Mousehole engaged there — sailing drifters, of course, for it was later that the first engine had been installed, in the "Edgar", at Mousehole, as I have said.

Sid himself was at Plymouth at that time, in the boat "Gleaner", P.Z. 139. He was just 14 years old, and went as cabin boy and cook. Permission could be given then for boys to leave school at 13 years of age to join the luggers. Some were enthusiastic in taking advantage of that permission, and, indeed, played a very useful part in the life aboard. My fisherman friend Jack Pender, Sid's elder brother, who has written an interesting book about his fishing days, his steamboating days, his fondly remembered yachting days and his experiences in the last war, left school at 13, and went to the North Sea in the newly-built lugger "Edgar". That was in 1903. Well, he is now over 92, and active still. Sid died just a short while ago.

With Sid in the "Gleaner" at Plymouth was my cousin, Harry Harvey (Susan Mary's brother), who was commonly known as "Butter". It is only recently that I have learnt from Jack the reason for that strange nickname. It seems that Harry was in the habit of softening his leather half-boots with butter instead of the usual "crease oil". Harry was a nice, quiet man, placid as many of the Mousehole fishermen were in those days.

The Plymouth herring season lasted from November to the middle of February, and was at its height at Christmas time. Before engaging upon the fishing in Bigberry Bay, off Plymouth, some boats liked to chance their luck at Padstow, for herring were still plentiful at times in the North Channel and Mount's Bay waters. My fisherman friend David spoke proudly to me of a monstrous catch there of 100 cran (28 stone), sold at 15 shillings per cran. But that was very much later than the time of the sailing luggers. I expect it was either in the "Ben-My-Chree", engine-driven, in which he first went to sea at the age of 15, in 1915, as cook, or, years later again, in his own new boat "Inter-Nos", P.Z. 46, sister-boat of Jack Pender's boat, the "Lyonesse", P.Z.81, built at approximately the same time, in 1930.

David was proud of his big catch at Padstow. He was surely proud also of the lady he met ashore there in that lovely village, the lady who became his wife.

Our sailing luggers, newly-rigged, spruce, set off for Plymouth and the herring season there in the month of November. Their departure was in the nature of a fête, even if for many on shore it could be regarded as a sad event. They would be away for over a month. But hopes were high, and a curious elation, which had pervaded the village the night before, bubbled up again in the hearts of the watchers on Mousehole pier as, in the morning, the boats cleared the harbour, and gathered speed. They bent to port or to starboard in response to the caress of the breeze. Soon the luggers would have passed the Shag Rock or the Dregman, according to the direction of the wind, and set their course for the Lizard Point, sixteen miles away. They would meet other luggers, perhaps, putting out from Newlyn or Porthleven, and in company with them slowly become invisible from the shore.

I see in imagination, in this village of Mousehole, the same setting out, the same adventurous enterprise, the same jubilation, centuries ago, in Elizabethan times, in a poorer but more rollicking age. And I seem to hear the feet of those fishermen, long ago.

> There is a beat
> Of other feet,
> Treading down the village street,
> Other voices, other songs,
> Other taverns, other throngs,
> And every single eye is bright
> With an Elizabethan light
> In the torch-lit streets to-night.
> They frolic to an old refrain —
> The herrings have come back again.
>
> Expectant now the luggers ride,
> Impatient for the morning tide.

The journey to Plymouth would take a full day, or more, less if the wind were favourable, and they would eventually reach the Barbican and go into their moorings at Sutton Pool, glad to recognise and meet their sister luggers from St. Ives and Looe and Mevagissey, already having made the journey.

My memory and my writing so far has been confined to the sailing luggers; but I do not think the pattern of fishing from the Barbican changed a great deal for quite a few years after engines — first paraffin (when sails were used as an auxiliary) and later petrol and diesel — were installed. It was then, certainly, a more rapid and less hazardous journey to the Barbican from the Cornish ports.

Fishing in Bigberry Bay was usually at night, and the catches landed in the early morning. At weekends our boats would remain in harbour. Upon occasion, however, especially if the fishing had been poor, a captain would be bold enough to defy the religious observance of the Sabbath, go out on the Saturday and land his fish next day, Sunday morning. Friendly relations could be seriously disturbed among the fishermen on these rare occasions, and the offending skipper would be told bluntly to "go down among the Lowestoft boats".

The same rigidity did not always obtain, however, and the sinners would receive a measure of clemency if they sought refuge, and perhaps pardon, in the ranks of the Salvation Army playing happily and vigorously on the pier.

During the night at sea sleep would be taken in snatches, except for the watcher on deck, as the luggers and the nets drifted slowly. I knew the bunks, and the stuffy smell of them, when I was young; but there were mattresses to sleep on, of course, sometimes straw mattresses, sometimes feather "ties". Life was spartan, hard, there was no disputing that. But our fishermen have always been used to that, and bear up stoically against it.

It must have been a brilliant sight in Bigberry Bay at night when the luggers had shot their nets, in company with the large numbers of East Country drifters which had come to Plymouth for the same herring fishery.

Of the life of the fishermen in the luggers at Plymouth before and after the turn of the century I have little knowledge. And there is scarcely anyone now to whom I can turn. I have just my own remembrance of stories related to me by my great-uncle Tom and a few of my older friends in the village.

The luggers would naturally have found it difficult at times to manoeuvre out from Sutton Pool, especially in adverse weather, and would prefer to land their catches and moor at Stonehouse, in Devonport, where there was easier access to the open sea, especially on a receding tide.

Life must have been similar in many ways to that of the later fishermen in their engined craft, but times were more difficult then, and pride in the luggers could not hide the fact that they suffered great hardship over long periods, especially in "dead weather" as they called it, when as much as a fortnight might elapse before they could be put to sea. However, our fishermen were skilled and adventurous, and very big catches of herring would be landed by them at the Barbican from time to time, easing their condition and enabling them to send more money home. It was all the happier for them if this occurred at Christmas time, when they would have enough money to take the trip home for a few days, travelling by rail. Christmas was in the very height of the herring season.

I have a story told me by Jack Pender's daughter, Sylvia, which will underline the hardship sometimes endured by the Cornish fishermen at the Barbican in those days. Sylvia has allowed me to tell it. Her grandfather was a fisherman at Plymouth, and eagerly expected home for Christmas. But the fishing up there had been poor for quite a time, and her grandfather had to make a sad decision.

It was customary for the fishermen at the Barbican to come home at Christmas, if possible, and to bring presents, especially for the children. Of course, there was Plymouth rock to bring home for them, but one present was regarded as special, being more or less of a rarity at that time.

It was a china-headed doll. Her grandfather had this doll happily in his mind to bring home for his daughter Nettie, Sylvia's mother. But the situation was such that he could not pay both for the trip home and the doll. There was not enough money. The trip home had to be abandoned, but he paid for and sent the doll, which was received by his daughter in tears for she would much rather that her father had come home. A greater poignancy was given to the tale by the revelation that in transit from Plymouth the doll's head had been broken in several places, and had to be sent back to be repaired.

I have no doubt that the fishermen in the luggers went ashore at times for a little entertainment, and on Sundays to the various places of worship. I shall have to supplement the small knowledge I have of these visits with those made later, and, I imagine, not so very different, by the fishermen in the engined drifters which had by that time supplanted the sailing craft.

I do know that my great uncle, Tom, in the days of the luggers, visited various places of worship ashore, and especially, I think, a chapel called the "Bethel". As I have written previously, he had a fine voice, which made him quite well-known round the Barbican. He made friends with a Mr. Mutton, a butcher there who supplied most of the luggers with meat, and to whom he would refer, in his stories to us, as "Maister Mutton". Later, my great-uncle, elderly, and long retired from the sea, went to stay with Mr. Mutton at Plymouth for a time. There was then no gas or electricity in the village of Mousehole, and my uncle, untutored in the use of these wonders, blew out the gas in his bedroom instead of turning it off. That was at Mr. Mutton's. Fortunately, he was discovered in time, in an unconscious state, but he very nearly succumbed. In telling us about it later, filling his pipe in his little cottage, he would begin with the words: "When I had that gas . . ."

I have no doubt that there were certain deviations of conduct at the Barbican at that time; but normally a very religious atmosphere obtained. There was a Bible in many of the cabins, and a short service, or prayers, at the casting of the nets. My fisherman friend Ned was telling me about his father, whom I remember quite well. In his lugger, the "Sweet Home", P.Z. 514, he was picking up a few crumpled leaves from his bible, which had fallen on to the floor of the cabin, and pushing them into the coal fire there. His son, much perplexed, remonstrated with him. "Why did you do that, Dad?" he asked. The answer came: "So that they shan't light their pipes with it." There was certainly a religious atmosphere there in the Sweet Home's cabin. That was actually in Mousehole harbour.

The same lugger had, of course, sailed often to the North Sea herring fishery, and presents, as I have said before, were brought home from there. At one time Ned's father bought a little ornament at Scarborough depicting a couple of orange sellers, for which he paid 18 pence. I expect it was in earthenware, but I am not sure of that. However, at home later someone bought it for 30 shillings. His daughter saw it later in a shop at Mousehole, and, with no intention of buying, I think, asked the price. She was told that she could have it for 12 guineas! Whereupon, having recognised the little article and knowing of the price put upon it as it lay in the market at Scarborough before her father had bought it, she expressed her anger at the ludicrously inflated price demanded in no uncertain terms.

The homecoming of the luggers was a memorable event in the village of Mousehole. I can remember standing on the Bank myself, as a youngster, watching the boats come round the Lizard, come into the Bay and make for Mousehole or Newlyn. It was indeed a good sight, especially if there was a fair breeze in the bay. And the watching fishermen — even their wives — would name the boats from afar, recognising every detail of their rig. It was uncanny, their ability to do this. I can hear now someone saying, "That's the Nellie. See her white foresail!"

My cousin Vaughan told me that his father, honouring a special request from some Mousehole fishermen, always painted the façade of his house at "Sunny Brea" white, as it would serve as a useful landmark for the returning luggers as they came into the Bay.

So they came home, one by one, sometimes in groups, the old luggers and their crew, some with a bit of money, others with very little. But times were to improve for them in the second, and especially the third, decade of this century, when engines had been installed, and there was less dependance on wind and tide. Sail was used only occasionally in the first few years of this change, as a source of extra power, for the early petrol and paraffin engines were not too efficient. Later, when powerful diesels were introduced, one could say that times had really changed, that the beautiful luggers were, in fact, luggers no longer, that they were just a dream, a happy dream, of the past.

The herring fishery at the Barbican continued as usual, however, and, as I have said, with happier prospects. Fishing then would not only be at nights, and access to the grounds, and return, became much easier.

I have spoken of my great interest in the life of our fishermen at Plymouth, and now, regretting that I have, for a time at least, to forget the old luggers, I can tell of it more fully, especially as I can get help from men much younger than those who were companions of my great-uncle Tom. And, of course, the boats at the Barbican will now be, most of them, engine-driven, and I shall be telling, not of the crews of the old luggers, but of the crews of the more modern engine-driven boats.

One might suppose that life on board the boats, sometimes moored up and unable to go to sea, was tedious and purposeless. To a degree that might have been so at times. But there were always plenty of things to do. There was the mending of nets, which in itself must often have taken quite a time, the stowing away of gear, the cleaning up and refurbishing on deck, the scrubbing-out of cabins, the lighting of the coal stoves, the cooking, the washing-up, the attention to the bunks — a host of necessary operations. And some of the gear might have had to be taken ashore at times to be immersed and freshly preserved.

I have no doubt that there was entertainment of a sort aboard many of the boats, too. Some young fishermen were skilful with mouth organs. I know that Chuggy had a concertina on the "Faithful", P.Z. 302, for instance; so that there could be quite good accompaniment to the many fine tenor and bass voices in the boats. There must have been at times something in the nature of a concert, in the quiet evenings, spreading to all other craft across the moorings.

And our fishermen, all of them, were very intelligent men. They could engage in intelligent conversation upon serious topics. I have been with them too often upon the Cliff at Mousehole to have any doubt about that. They had spent their lives in frail craft, alone in wide waters. There was time and occasion for thought in that immensity.

I would venture to say that they talked about more important things than many do today. I can see them, some with their pipes, some quietly chewing their twist-tobacco, talking placidly together as the evenings drew in.

Always I have wondered about the youngsters there in the Barbican, the boys who had enthusiastically joined the herring fleet. They went as cabin boys. They did the cooking, cleaned out the cabins, sometimes thoroughly with scrubbing brush, hot water and soda, and employed themselves usefully in all sorts of ways. I think that in the main they enjoyed themselves, and had no regret for the initial decision they had made.

The food for the fishermen was ordered and sent aboard — usually a week's supply. Jack Pender has written about that in his book, and from his account of the "steak and onions for Saturday, the roast for Sunday, and the stew for Monday" I should say that at times the crews did themselves very well. Sometimes, if the catches had been good and prices satisfactory, a really good big joint of meat would be bought and salted in — placed in what was called the "harness cask". I think that meat must have tasted good. I expect too that at sea, and even in the port, lines were cast, especially for mackerel and pollack.

Well, of course, they couldn't stay in the boats all the time, and at weekends they went ashore and enjoyed themselves as best they could. On Saturdays some went to the first house of the Palace Theatre — sitting "up in the Gods" — for only sixpence; to the Royal Theatre also, or the Queen's. Others, later in the day, went down to the Hippodrome at Devonport.

Let me not enquire too closely into the diversions of the young men at the Barbican, free of the drifters for a moment. There was very little money for a spree. There were rough spots and rough characters about close to the moorings, and some youngsters would often venture no further than the top of Looe Street, from which there would be a straight and rapid descent to the boats if they were pestered. Some of the fishermen must have had a few drinks, and, occasionally, a sailor would be helped back aboard. Of amatory encounters I have been told, but of those sought or chanced upon I have nothing to say. It were best that in this story such aberrations were left untold. Upon the whole it was a life of sobriety and fair amusement.

On Sundays the main bulk of the Cornish fishermen — those who were churchgoers — went to the King Street Methodist Chapel, very conspicuous there, in their knitted guernseys. A lot went to the Salvation Army, others to the Congress Hall in the Octagon for the evening service, or to King Street Wesleyan Chapel. And some, still more religiously inclined perhaps, would form a group and hold a short service with hymns and prayers for the patients at the City Hospital.

I feel, sadly, at this stage of my story, that I cannot say much more about the herring fishery and the life of our men at the Barbican. Whatever details, outside my own knowledge, I have been able to gather, have been given me by sailors in the more modern engine-driven craft. I have stolen from their experience, and to them I am very grateful. I had, perforce, to forget just for a while the old luggers, because the story of their life at the Barbican was too far in the past for me to remember, or for others to tell me of. I felt in any case that the tenor of their life there at that time, long ago now, would have been more or less the same as that of those more modern fishermen from whom I have borrowed.

So I will leave the more modern boats at Plymouth. They would soon be leaving, at the end of the season — somewhere in February — to come home and fit out for the mackerel season, or long-lining, or pilchard-driving, nearer home.

Return to the Barbican would come again, later, but it is regrettable that the herring shoals gradually disappeared off the coasts of Cornwall and Devon.

X
Disasters at Sea

As I have said before in my story, sudden gales could spring up around our coasts and reach alarming proportions in a very short time. In recent times the winds blow frequently and heavily from the northwest and northeast, but they came mainly from the southwest when I was a boy, and a boat was lucky indeed if fishing not too deep and could put into Scilly for safety. Tides were dangerous too, very dangerous at times, and rounding the Land's End or the Lizard to come into our bay could be hazardous in the extreme, especially if then driving before the wind in a heavy gale.

Looking outward across the Bay from Mousehole towards the shallows at the Malpas Buoy and Carn Lullow, during a southern gale, one could see from the shore, and be appalled at the tumult of the water there, the terrific wash where no boat could live.

Sea-mists, too, were a source of great danger, as sometimes they would be thick enough to limit visibility to a few yards only. Then was it that the extraordinary ability of our fishermen to know where they were, to recognise the sounds of the shore, the baleful sighings, could be their salvation.

In spite of the perilous conditions our fishermen had sometimes to face, it is a tribute to their skill at sea and to the stoutness of their craft that accidents were very rare indeed. Disaster struck at least two of our luggers, however, with fatal consequences, and with less serious effect in the case of some others. Of all these of which I have knowledge I will try in the next few pages to give some account.

The broad facts concerning the lugger "Jane", P.Z. 26, have always been known to me, but I am indebted to the Western Morning News, in their edition of the tenth of October, 1980, the centenary of her tragic voyage, for extra details which cannot fail to stir the emotions of my readers.

In the dark early hours of the morning, on October 7th, 1880, the lugger "Jane", bound home from Whitby, rounded the Lizard in a terrific southeast gale and made for Penzance. Other boats behind her, fearing the increasing violence of the wind, had remained in shelter either at Brixham or Plymouth. But the "Jane" continued, as did three luggers ahead of her — the "Percy", the "Mary", and the "Dart". These three, miraculously, rode the appalling troughs in the shallows outside Penzance harbour, and berthed in safety, just as dawn broke.

The "Jane" failed to make the harbour. She was struck by a gigantic wave in attempting the turn into the gaps, withstood that battering bravely, only to be struck again, fatally, by others rebounding fiercely from the pier. She capsized, was driven shoreward, and in that maelstrom reduced to matchwood. All the crew perished.

The bodies of two of the crew — the skipper, John Thomas Wallis, aged 29, and a youngster, William Tonkin, aged only 16, were never found. Other members of the crew were: William John Williams, aged 29; Frederick Curtis and Nicholas Richards, both aged 22; Peter John Harvey, a youngster of 16, and Philip Charles Worth, just a boy of 15 years.

Some wondered later why those luggers made for Penzance harbour at all. They had no choice. The baulks were down at Mousehole, and there was only the small harbour then at Newlyn, tidal, and totally unsuitable for receiving them.

It had not been a very successful season for the "Jane" in the North Sea. Her total takings had been just over £60.

She came to disaster a long time ago, but there are still relatives of her crew in Mousehole and nearby. The widow of William John Williams, known as Aunt Tammy, lived to the age of 103, and died in 1950. I have very pleasant memories of Johnnie Williams her son, and father of a lady still resident in the village — Janie, Mrs. Sidney Pender.

"*Running for Harbour*", *by Jack Pender*

There are many relatives, too, of the ill-fated lugger "Emmeline". She was lost with all hands coming home from Scarborough in the early years of the century. Her skipper was Abe Madron, great grandfather of the present fishermen, Jimmy and Joe Madron of Mousehole. Whether she ran ashore on the Goodwins in a gale or heavy mist, or whether she was in collision with another craft, is not really known. The last thing known of her was that she had put into Dover for bread. A foresail with her number was recovered from the beach at Shoreham in Sussex, and that remains the sole relic of the disaster.

There was one lucky member of the Emmeline's crew. His name was Sidney Oliver. He was quite well-known to me. He left the lugger at Scarborough, or at Lowestoft, where she had put in for a while, and decided to come home by rail. Why Sidney left the boat I do not know. Was he afraid of the return trip? Had he pressing business at home? Did he have a premonition of disaster? I cannot tell. Whatever the cause, he was, miraculously, not involved in the tragic fate of his companions.

And the Madron family, always skilful at sea, and having experienced other sad losses, carry valiantly on.

The lugger 'Weatherall", P.Z. 1, was run down by a Brixham trawler, and lost, near the Longships. It was a tragic encounter, for one of the crew, William Humphries, lost his life. He was uncle to Mrs. Ladner, in the newspaper shop at Mousehole. I have no details of this disaster, but it must have affected the captain (William Henry Polgrean) very much indeed, for he never went to sea again. He went to London and joined the police. He recognised me, years later, and waved to me from a river police-launch as I stood looking over Westminster Bridge. I was a student then.

The "Orlando", P.Z. 495, coming home from Plymouth, went to the aid of the "Emblem", P.Z. 575. The "Emblem" had carried her mast away, and the "Orlando" stood by. In the thick misty weather the two boats lost contact with each other for a while, and the "Orlando" searching desperately for her companion, had the misfortune to come upon her suddenly, and ran into her, with tragic consequences. The "Orlando" sank, but not before the men of her crew had jumped aboard the "Emblem". One boy, called Brownfield ("Brownie", as I knew him), heard the crash of the collision in his bunk, and came on deck as the boats pulled apart. He went to loose the punt, but the punt was lashed to her supports. However he went back to the cabin for a knife and was successful in cutting her adrift. He was rescued by the crew of the "Emblem".

Fortunately, no lives were lost, and Captain Jenkin of the "Orlando", known as "Spoose", must have been thankful for that. But his own boat had gone down, and with her the £40 which he had put for safety under the pillow in his bunk.

The "Emblem", of which I have just spoken, owned by Johnnie and Eddie Hicks, was rather unfortunate later on. She slipped her moorings and drifted out of the harbour in March, 1914. There was a bad running tide at the time, and strong surf in the gaps. The other boats in the harbour were straining violently at their chains. Jack Hicks, son of the captain, ran frantically to the pierhead with the intention of jumping on board as the boat went through the gaps. He was, fortunately, restrained. But the "Emblem" ran ashore close by, just off Carn Topna, near the Bell Rock and Point Set, and was a total wreck. She was bought by Captain Sincock, who transferred a lot of her valuable pitchpine timbers to his house at the "Villa". Her engine was taken out and transferred later to the Hicks's new boat, the "Emblem", P.Z. 26. She was, unfortunately, not insured. I think if she had been it would have been with the "Cornish Insurance" of the time, which went bankrupt.

The second "Emblem", P.Z. 26, seemed to have a jinx on her too, for she caught fire 20 miles southwest of the Wolf. It was a desperate situation, but her crew were rescued by the "Orion", standing near by.

The lugger "Kite", owned by the Downing family, slipped her moorings and floated out of the harbour at Mousehole. That was well before the turn of the century. She ran into the back of the pier, and was a total wreck. Not all the boats were insured at that time, but the "Kite" was, luckily enough, and the insurance duly paid to the owners.

The lugger "Telephone", P.Z. 230, belonging to the Pentreath family of Mousehole, was in collision with a sailing-vessel. It was difficult at the time to establish which of the two craft bore the chief blame for the accident, and there was a Court Case to decide the issue. Unfortunately, the Court held the crew of the "Telephone" responsible. It was a sad decision, but, happily for them, the Court costs were paid by a kind gentleman of the village.

I must mention finally the mysterious loss of the "Arethusa", belonging to Mr. J.F. Ladner, brother to two of her crew who perished — Richard Ladner and Madron Ladner, and brother-in-law to two of the others — Thomas Cotton and Harry Harvey.

It was thought that she must have been run down in misty weather by another boat somewhere this side of the "Wolf". But nothing was ever found. Only a vague rumour persisted afterwards that a death-bed confession of culpability had been made.

The boats I have mentioned faced accident or disaster in various ways. But the "Hopeful", P.Z. 634, a square-sterned former lugger, ended her day in no tragic crcumstances. She was beached by her owner, Tom Jim Matthews, at the foot of the War Memorial in Mousehole harbour, and broken up.

Tom Jim was a lion of a man, heavily-bearded, massive. He wielded his sledge-hammer with devastating effect upon the "Hopeful" — tore her timbers apart, and pushed them up the difficult and winding slope to his home at "Coronation Villas" in a wheelbarrow. Even the wheelhouse he transported in the same way, and erected it at the entrance to his home, for all to see. It stood there for many years, a vivid and touching reminder of his old boat. Why did he do it? Well, his fishing days — which had been highly successful — were over, and I have heard it said that the "Hopeful" was lightly built, not a strong boat, in spite of her size.

I have said very little about the boats we called "half-and-halfers". They were in size between the big luggers and the pilchard-drivers. They were useful boats, more suited to tackle all seasons, perhaps, than the big luggers. One half-and-halfer I particularly remember, because she must feature in my list of accidents. She was the "Agnes", P.Z. 334, and belonged to the Downing family. She was about 30 feet long. Coming from the Wolf with a shot of pilchards aboard she encountered heavy mist, struck a rock just under Tater Dhu, and sank. Her crew were taken off by Tom Bones in his small craft, the "Daisy", but she could not be recovered. Fortunately, her floats came up, and her nets were saved.

Tom Bones's boat, the "Daisy", was called in jest the "marinated pilchard boat", because his wife did a good trade in marinated pilchards.

I believe I might be wrong in calling the "Agnes" a half-and halfer, and that she was in fact a pilchard-driver. Still, let me keep what I have written.

I have no doubt that there were accidents to other boats over the years, but I have knowledge only of those of which I have spoken, and which occurred, most of them, within the present century. Life must have been vastly more precarious for the sailors in the old open-decked craft of the past, and, doubtless, they sometimes met with disaster.

XI
Dangers in the Harbour

The harbour itself could be a dangerous place. There were formerly rails of wrought iron at the edge of the Cliff, and along the quays. I cannot think why the former were ever uprooted. They were strong, deeply embedded, and had been there ever since I could remember, and for goodness knows how many years before that. It would surely have sufficed to have put, for greater safety, a central rail. I have noticed that the present rails have been bent frequently, and in strength and appearance seem to be much inferior to those they have replaced.

But the old rails did not prevent accidents altogether. I know of several children who fell over the Cliff Road into the harbour below — a drop of about 25 feet — with only minor injuries. In fact, my younger brother fell over, and was unharmed. My dog too, startled by the sudden shaking of a cloth from the paper-shop. And the dog, "Caesar", suffered no injury.

My friend Mac fell over as he emerged hurriedly, guiltily perhaps, from Joe Rowe's shop, into which he had ventured to buy a packet of Woodbines — a small paper-packet of five, costing 2d. in those days — for his older pals outside, who had not dared to enter themselves. He was fortunate to land upon a small patch of sand between the blue-elvan rocks below, and was unharmed. He laughed when he recalled the full facts of his adventure to me recently.

Walford Hockin went over at a more dangerous point, just opposite the entrance to my uncle's bark-house. He survived the fall, suffering only an injury to his upper lip which left a permanent mark.

John Cotton, a schoolboy coming in from sea, fell over in front of the Cliff newspaper-shop. He sustained rather serious injury to his back, and was forced to lie in bed for a period.

Sid Waters, aged about 8 to 10 years, fell over, like Mac, in front of the Ship Inn. He swung out on the rails — a common practice then among the boys — and lost his grip. He was lucky to fall clear of the rocks below, and was uninjured. He was seen to fall by Dick Ladner at the paper-shop, and was helped by him up over the steps to the Cliff.

Pentreath Hudson, Lizzie Deeble's son, fell over as a small boy. His injuries were serious, and he was taken to Penzance hospital with a fractured skull. There he was fortunate to have the attention of a skilful surgeon on holiday in the district, and made a good recovery.

John Dennis, a "jouster", leaving his pony and cart for a moment and resting a bag of flour against the rails, went over just opposite the seats leading down to the North Pier. He was seriously injured, and had to have his arm amputated.

A visiting drunk was seen to emerge from the "Ship" and reel towards the rails. He went over in somersaults according to one witness, and was severely shaken. He was helped up the steps to his lodgings, but appeared at the Inn later in the evening for a few more pints. I have never known the gentleman's name.

It is astonishing, but I have no record of any fatal injury as a result of falling over the Cliff.

In the harbour itself there was really less danger than upon the Cliff road, for most of us could swim at a very early age, and were well acquainted with the hazards to be encountered there. Nevertheless, I can tell of one very sad occurrence that was fatal, and another that might have been unless quick help was at hand.

Archie Blewett, Bill Blewett's young brother, boarding the luggers moored alongside the steps on the North Pier, slipped and fell between the pilchard-driver "Sunbeam" and another boat. He rose to the surface, but could get no grip on the smooth hulls, and was drowned. He was recovered, but frantic efforts to revive him were of no avail. His pals had run up to get help from the fishermen on the Cliff, but that help, it seems, came too late to save Archie.

Harry Worth fell over the side of the mackerel-driver "Our Maggie", with his iron hoop and drill in his hands; but this time help was close at hand. Nicky Paine Rowe, Hilda's father, jumped in promptly and held him safely until he was pulled aboard the "Maggie" — with his hoop and drill still in his hands!

As I have said, we became expert scullers early on, and we would sometimes borrow a punt and go fishing on what was called the "drethan" — a patch of water with a sandy bottom halfway to the Island. The "drethan" was a famous place for pollack. For bait we could get pilchards from my father's cellar or from some pilchard-driver lying alongside the pier. It would not be long before we felt a bite, for in those days there was no lack of fish inshore. In fact, there were so many chads and bream that we could fill a fair-sized basket in a couple of hours. There was often a bite every minute. Sometimes my father would take us fishing a bit further out, beyond the Shag Rock, on some shallows at that corner of the Island. He was expert in baiting the hooks, with cleverly-cut thin strips from the pilchards. Sometimes, if we were not getting bites — and this was rare — or if the punts a little way off seemed to be doing better than we were, we put out what we called "smack" — that is, quite a lot of broken-up bait, to lure the fish away from our rivals. It was unfair, of course, but they would probably have done the same to us if the positions had been reversed.

I must go back to the harbour where I said there could be danger. In fact, it is surprising that accidents were so few. There were stones everywhere, in the harbour and on the rocks, and stone-throwing was rife. My brother in his book has spoken of the pleasure we experienced in jerking thin flat stones, specially chosen, over the level water, and watching their ricochetting flight. That was innocent amusement, indeed. But stone-throwing was far from innocent at times, and in quarrels heads were often "cut abroad". Two boys would face each other, stones in hand, and the warning might come from one, menacingly, "I'll cut you down!" In the majority of cases, I am glad to say, the confrontation would go no further.

But stone-throwing was certainly very dangerous at times. Stones seemed to be coming from everywhere at a given moment, and, rarely, a boy lost the sight of an eye.

There was great accuracy, too, if the thrower were determined. It was a favourite sport, out on the rocks, during bathing-time, to fix a fair-sized stone, which we called a "picket", on the top of a prominent rock, say twenty yards away, and pelt it with stones until one lucky shot struck it from its perch. On these occasions bathers nearby might be in considerable danger from the flying stones. Indeed, I have myself seen a swimmer emerge, having been struck on the mouth, to inflict deserved punishment upon the rash perpetrator of his injury.

Sometimes a shag, or a cormorant, those marvellously-neat divers, would appear on the surface of the water, inside the harbour, or outside, and, I am sorry to say, would be pelted with stones by some unthinking boys, and even adults, to the accompaniment of the traditional cry: "Trainygoat! Trainygoat!" That was the word we used for the shags.

This cruel practice stemmed possibly from the idea that these birds, which were certainly numerous at times, made unacceptable inroads upon the inshore fish. Today, injured birds are taken, tenderly, to the Mousehole Hospital for Birds, especially by the young. The originators of that Hospital, the ladies Dorothy, Phyllis and Mary Yglesias, who came with their mother from their London home in St. John's Wood, just before the first World War, to the village they grew to love, must have been gladdened, as they grew older, by this stupendous change in conduct, for which they had surely been largely responsible.

I am sure that the shags were usually clever enough to escape the pelting, and for that I am very grateful, when I remember it all.

Breton fishermen from their crabbers in Newlyn sometimes came with shotguns to attack the shags and cormorants, especially in the vicinity of our Island. It was a rather vile practice, we thought, as we grew older; but there was some excuse for them, perhaps, for they were very poor indeed. They even came frequently over our rocks to collect limpets in their buckets for consumption.

I have mentioned the ships' spars which reached down from the Cliff Road to the harbour floor below, which we called the "Por". Down these we slid, rapidly, when there were no nets placed upon them to dry. It was a pleasurable exercise, and no danger seemed attached to it, skilful as we were. Looking back, however, I remember that in the narrow slits of the wood along the spars some mischievous boys would insert thin pieces of slate. It seems to me now that a rapid descent in those circumstances might have been very dangerous indeed. But nothing serious seems to have happened.

I shudder today, when I see quite young boys, legs slung over the far edge of the north pier, baiting their hooks and casting out their lines. And I am sure that some of them cannot swim. The slightest push, it seems, would be disastrous for them. If I were young, and they fell, I could rescue them all right. But not now. I am old, and those boys are far more secure than I imagine.

We were always moving about in punts, sometimes borrowed ones, sometimes our own, which had been used in putting fishermen aboard their boats. One day our punt was moored with a painter made fast to the stern of the pilchard-driver "Mizpah", P.Z. 49. She was among the downtown boats, and belonged to the Praed family. There were two brothers with me, one older and one younger, and it was high tide in the harbour. I must have been about eight or nine years old at the time. My younger brother, Alan, in the after-part of the punt, went overboard, and sank. He couldn't swim. My elder brother, Walter, was up in the bows loosening the painter in case we had to move quickly. Alan wasn't coming up. We were terrified at the length of time which elapsed before he suddenly shot up again near me at the stern, and I pulled him aboard. I shudder now when I think of it, and how we might have had to go home to my mother with the news that Alan had drowned. I know that in remembering I might possibly exaggerate the time my brother was under that water, but I still think that he must have become entangled in some ropes or chains on the bottom.

That accident could have been tragic, but there was another, when I was much younger, that was quite frightening, too. We had a pilchard-driver called the "Charles". I forget her number. She was moored up against the North Pier, and it was again high tide. My father was descending a chain ladder, with me in his arms, to the lugger, in order to put some extra cement ballast in her bottom. He slipped on a rung of the ladder, and fell, holding me still, between the "Charles" and the pier. There was not a great width of water there, and, of course, that could narrow rapidly. However, we came to the surface safely, and my great-uncle Tom pulled me aboard. Uncle Tom worked on the "Charles". We had to walk home, "sumping wet", across the Cliff, to the consternation, and amusement too, of the fishermen walking up and down there.

That walking up and down was a notable and constant feature of the village life when I was a boy, especially when the weather was poor and the boats could not put to sea. The Cliff, and I have no doubt, the Wharf too, was a sort of forum, where intelligent conversation occurred, discussions on all manner of serious topics. It formed one of what I might call the "tableaux" of which I hope to speak now — little pictures of the village life — as I move, rather tiredly, I must confess, closer to the conclusion of my book.

I doubt if there was much talk among them of fishing matters. It was for them a sort of relaxation, a few moments to speak of other things, a kind of school for them perhaps, for, as I have said, they were men of great intelligence, eager to learn. There was a certain pathos in the fact that they were there so often, for most of them had little money to travel. They did walk up the lane and into the country regularly, some of them, when they were older. They were religious and likeable men. There might, occasionally, have been rougher groups here, on the Cliff, when the young ladies of the village would be afraid to pass, but I think the fears of the latter were often exaggerated.

XII
Magic Nights at Sea

I remember beautiful nights in the Summer months, in the sailing time; halcyon nights when the sea was as calm as a lake, and the Bay swarming with pilchards. Our luggers would put out in the late afternoon, some to the inner reaches of the Bay, others more to the westward. They would be joined by luggers from Newlyn, Porthleven and St. Ives — all come in pursuit of the shoals. They would take parallel positions, skilfully, and drift with the tide after casting their nets. And later, when the night closed in, the Bay would be lit up, like a city afloat.

I have been out there myself, more than once, in that expectant assembly, in the wonder of those quiet floating nights.

During the long wait for the haul, it was customary to fish for mackerel, which would be boiled in the cabin for supper. I was a good sailor, not subject to sea-sickness, and so I could enjoy those mackerel in the strange, stuffy atmosphere of the cabin. If the hour were late, I would be advised to go into a bunk and sleep a little, in that still stuffier and confined space.

At the moment when the skipper felt that it was time to haul in the nets, one of the crew would lean over the side of the boat, with a broom-handle perhaps, and agitate the water. This was called "brimming". If the phosphorescence was truly agleam, it would be considered a favourable sign — that the pilchards were there — and the nets would slowly be hauled in.

In the return to harbour, in the late hours, or in the early morning, a slight mist might be encountered, and the fishermen made more aware of their position close to the coast by the rattling of iron rings upon the pier.

The slow entry of the pilchard-drivers into the harbour was an unforgettable sight. To the watchers on the pier would come, perhaps, the lazy flapping of a sail, the splashing of an oar, voices. The luggers were coming in. Out of the night then, suddenly, a shadow would emerge, in the shape of a boat, and others would follow, in weird procession. It was like an unfolding dream.

The magic would reach its climax for the watchers as they gazed upon the shining masses of pilchards on lucky decks. There might be thousands of them, tens of thousands, several "lasts", gleaming like silver, some still in the nets, to be unmeshed later, with helping hands, in the morning, on the harbour floor. A "last" was 10,000 fish.

Some boats would come bravely in, with "hatches laid". That signified to the watchers that their holds were empty, that for them it had been an unlucky and unprofitable night.

Buyers, or their representatives, would be on the pier-head, noting if the boats normally attached to them had been successful or not. They would sometimes try to capture the custom of other boats by shouting down and offering bigger prices than were then current. I can myself remember one buyer — for some reason unknown to me antagonistic to my father, a buyer himself — leaning over the harbour rail and shouting down to a boat: "Have you come in to sell? Twenty-five shillings a thousand!" That was a rather higher price than was normal at the time.

Some of the drifters came in very late, and if the tide were low, would anchor offshore until the morning.

I stand upon that pierhead again, in imagination, as I write, and it is not only the luggers that I see. I see faces that have gone; fresh young faces of boys and girls I knew, surging forward eagerly to the rails to watch the magic entry, in the magic night.

XIII
What became of the Luggers?

I sit in my chair this evening, knowing that I shall soon now have to complete my story of the beautiful luggers. Much of what I have written is factual. But I was conscious, always, as I wrote, of a certain glory investing them and their crews; a glory that was dimmed at moments, perhaps, by suffering, but made brighter still by heroic effort and religious faith. I wrote as far as I was able of a fascinating, age-long calling. Of high romance. It would be good, perhaps, for those today who have little knowledge of, or regard for, the past, to look back, and think, and wonder.

What became of the luggers? It is a question that might well be asked. I have no knowledge to answer that question in detail. Some were admired by gentlemen who bought them and used them as yachts; others had engines installed and continued fishing for quite a time, to be supplanted later by craft more suitable for the modern style of fishing. Some were sold to other ports, and plied their old trade there, with different crews. As for the ultimate destination of them all, I have no reliable record. But I have a list which might interest my readers, supplied to me by my fisherman friends Johnny Drew and Jack Worth. This list includes not only some of the old luggers, but also many of the later engine-driven craft, and shows to what places they were sold. I have, of course, already indicated the fate of some of the luggers, and they are therefore not included in this list, which is restricted really to only a few boats.

Ben-My-Chree	sold to	Howth, finished up in Ardglass
Bonnie Lad	,, ,,	Howth
Bonnie Lass	,, ,,	Bournemouth
Boy Ben	,, ,,	Porthleven
Boy Don	,, ,,	Jersey
Children's Friend	,, ,,	Fishguard
Comfort	,, ,,	Howth
Edgar	,, ,,	Plymouth
Girl Joyce	,, ,,	Ilfracombe
Girl Stella	,, ,,	Gosport
Golden Sunset	,, ,,	Plymouth
Heather Glen	,, ,,	Gosport
Ibex	,, ,,	Howth

Inter Nos	,,	,,	Falmouth
Lyonesse	,,	,,	Weymouth
Nellie Jane	,,	,,	Sunderland
Penzer	,,	,,	Gosport
Radiant Morn	,,	,,	Howth
Smiling Morn	,,	,,	Plymouth
Sweet Home	,,	,,	Newlyn
Two Boys	,,	,,	Gosport
William	,,	,,	Newlyn

My story has been mainly of the fishermen of my own village. But the same story could have been told of the fishermen of the lovely village of Newlyn, just two miles away; of the St. Ives men, of those of Porthleven, Mevagissey and Looe. They put out on the same hazardous voyages — to Ireland, the North Sea, Plymouth — in the same decked and undecked boats. They encountered the same treacherous winds, endured the same hardships, led the same life, aboard and on shore. So that when I sailed with the Mousehole men I sailed with them also. They were always in my mind.

XIV
The Galas

In my dream the luggers sail away, and I stand, a boy five or six years old, in front of my grandfather's cottage on the Cliff at Mousehole. Lilies are behind me in the narrow plot, and fragrant pinks. It is some time in July. Trumpets are sounding downtown, somewhere in the narrow streets, and a moving procession is glimpsed in the gaps between the houses. The music comes, now faint, now loud. The Paul and St. Just bands are playing. The village is in festive mood for the Wesleyan Sunday School "treat". It is Gala Day.

I am in the midst of a concourse of people lining the streets, expectant, and someone is holding my hand.

There comes a sudden and more penetrating burst of music, and banners appear, coming round the bend near Susan Mary's — one leading the marching young men and children, the other in front of the girls.

The banners are strikingly beautiful. They were painted by local artists. One pictures Jesus as a Shepherd, and bears the motto: "God is our Strength". The other shows the infant Jesus with his Mother — an open Bible upon her lap. She is giving the Child instruction in the Scriptures. Underneath is written: "Thy Word is a lamp unto our path". The colours on this banner are rich indeed, especially the red gown and cap and blue blouse in which Mary is clothed.

The Wesleyan banners can be seen in St. Clement's Chapel, spread upon the walls on either side of the choir stalls, upstairs. They are fortunately placed, in a striking position.

I see my grandfather at the head of the procession. He is like an Old Testament prophet. I think it is a moment of triumph for him, old stern Wesleyan as he is, adhering resolutely to the rules of conduct in which he had been brought up, rigidly faithful to a creed that could be narrow and bigoted in the extreme, but which nevertheless laid the basis for honourable conduct, for something that was good.

The procession went to the head of the North Pier, and there, after three jubilant cheers, the National Anthem was sung.

I was in that procession myself a few years later, when I had grown up a little. The preparation for it was for us a treat in itself. It all comes back to me. We assembled, boys and girls, in the old Schoolroom, now St. Clement's Hall, which was our Sunday School at that time. I feel aware, today, of the kindly help given us, the consideration shown by the cheerful Sunday School teachers.

It is strange indeed, the pleasure we took in the simple proceedings. We strove, the boys, each of us, to secure a flag for the march through the village. There seemed to be no end of them in the Schoolroom, and we chose the prettiest ones we could find. A few years later we were to grow envious of the young men and girls who were allowed to carry staffs with gay ribbons at the top. We wanted to be grown-up too.

Hoisting our flags happily, we joined in such a procession as I have described, ending in a regal passage across the Cliff and down to the head of the North Pier. Here the march was by no means over. There was a long way to go, as the bands struck up gaily again and the marching columns started on their long way to Newlyn town.

I was still too young to walk such a distance, and went with others up the lane to Paul, thence to a big field at Chywoone which the Jarvis family had allowed us to use, each summer, for our Gala, which we called "Park".

There was the smell of the grass, and a big tea being prepared for us, with plenty of cakes, and jelly and cream. There were strawberries too, plenty of them, bought from gaily-painted light carts from Penzance. Each boy and girl was presented with the traditional big, round saffron bun — and saffron buns from Chirgwin's were good in those days. Some of us wrapped them in large red handkerchiefs, to take home, tying the four corners together.

We had races organised, and there were cycle races for the older folk attending. It was much later, when I was about twelve, perhaps, that in that sweet-smelling field of Chywoone I won my first race. It was against a boy from a sporting family near St. Ives. I ran in my ordinary clothes and sandshoes then, but he looked confident, and formidable indeed, in his full track regalia — vest and shorts and spiked shoes, and even cork handgrips, which I had never seen before. I beat him, easily.

We were all waiting, in that field, for the procession that had gone to Newlyn Town, and would now be slowly mounting the long and steep Paul Hill. It was a breath-taking moment for us when the first loud blast of the cornets was heard. Soon the marchers appeared over the brow of the hill, and came triumphantly up the long drive into the field.

Of course, for the older marchers and visitors there were distractions, chief of which, perhaps, was the so-called "kissing-ring". They formed a circle, young men and women, alternately placed. A maiden ranging outside the circle would boldly tap the shoulder of a young man of her choice, and a furious pursuit would ensue, to be ended in capture, inevitably, and a kiss. It was a repetition of an age-old pursuit, reaching back into Classical times.

We walked home through the stiled fields, through the standing corn, along well-kept paths. We made laughing inroads into the barley and oats as we passed. Nature was sweet and quiet and beautiful around us then. The hedges were intact, separating the small fields. There were no barriers across the stiles. It was truly rural. It was to be a long time before the machine would supplant the horse. There is not the same pleasure today in walking through those fields, if that were indeed possible, unkept and almost undiscoverable as the paths now are.

The walk to Newlyn seems to have been abandoned a few years before the first World War. After that the procession went from Mousehole straight to Chywoone — up the lane through the village of Paul and thence to the Gala field. I have been told that later on the festivities took place in a field on the left after leaving Paul.

The Primitive Methodists held their Gala about a week later than the others, and their festivities followed much the same line. It was Gala time in the village again, and a similar flagged procession made its way happily through the streets. I have never quite understood why the "Little Chapel", as we called it, broke away from the Wesleyans. I think it had something to do with strongly-held differing religious views on either drinking or smoking. Whatever the case, a certain mild antagonism persisted between the two, and expressed itself in a strange way at Gala time. Some of the Wesleyans would kill snails on the eve of the Primitives' gala, in the superstitious and nasty hope that it would bring rain upon the morrow and mar their festivities. And the Primitives, some of them, would ill-wish the Wesleyans in the same way upon the eve of their gala. Fortunately, their efforts were often in vain.

XV
The Chapel & Revival Services

Cornish chapels are not the most attractive of buildings often, and they certainly compare unfavourably in that respect with our beautiful churches. But whatever there is to displease — and there is very little indeed — in the Wesleyan Chapel at Mousehole, can well be forgotten, for the richly-coloured windows spread a glory over the whole interior. They are beautiful. They reflect the strong religious feelings and generosity of those who put them there.

We had a pew in the Chapel when we were young, quite close to a lovely window given by my father — a representation of Holman Hunt's painting: "I am the Light of the World". My father sat at the end of the pew, against the corridor, on Sundays, and passed Rowntree's gums up to us at intervals during the sermon. There were quite a lot of giggles, especially when some over-enthusiastic member of the congregation would cry out "Hallelujah" or "Praise the Lord", and much-feared pinches from my father as the pew shook with more pronounced laughter. However, my father was apt to nod and almost fall asleep at times, so that our punishment was not continuous. We tried as best we could, each of us, not to sit close to him. My grandfather's pew was up in front, to the right of us, and he had a seat upstairs in the gallery too, to which we retreated at times to feel more secure in our detachment from the proceedings, which we were really too young to understand properly at that time.

One thing we did understand, and that was the magnificent singing of the Choir and the Congregation. Both our Chapels were renowned for that. The wonderful hymns, the wonderful words in them, held our attention, in spite of ourselves, and thenceforth for ever had a place in our lives.

As my brother has indicated in his book, the evening services in the Chapel were more heavily attended than the morning services. They were presided over by the regular Ministers of the Wesleyan Circuit. Some of the latter were fine men, and notable preachers. I remember especially two of them — the Rev. Simpson Hall and the Rev. Sidney Lawson. My mother, who played the harmonium in the Chapel when she came as a young lady from Padstow to teach in the Wesleyan School at Mousehole, greatly admired the former, a rather frail man, whose quaint, attractive manner and high intelligence made a striking impact upon his audience. He was broad in his Christian outlook, very broad. He held that there were many roads to ultimate salvation; that it did not matter overmuch upon which we embarked, so long as, in his own words, we "got there in the end". That was the much-loved "Simpie", as we called him.

The other Minister, the Rev. Lawson, I shall always remember, and honour, for he introduced me, as a young man, to the poetry of Francis Thompson, to "The Hound of Heaven", that poem of vital religious content and extraordinary beauty of language which I would place as the supreme poetic expression of this century.

There were local preachers too, at times, many of them devoted men, not always highly educated, but driven by an impulse that was surely good, to stand in the pulpit and speak with power, often against the evils of the times. There were also some very rigid in their views, sticking to the literal truth of the Bible — fundamentalists, shall I call them — requiring always what they called "The Gospel" to be preached. They would sometimes call for a Prayer Meeting at the conclusion of the morning service — certainly somewhat of an ordeal for the worshippers, following upon what had often been a dull and lengthy address before. They would not permit of any interruption of these prayer-meetings, even when perhaps some noted organist had been invited to give a short and much-anticipated recital. One local preacher who erred in this respect, and caused considerable resentment as a result, was, I think, called "Googe" "Googe! Who's Googe?" I heard an irate and disappointed man complain, outside the Chapel. It was a stinging comment.

Most of these local preachers, however, as I have said, were very religious, thoughtful men, and I remember them with pleasure. Some had peculiarities of manner that caused us much amusement. One man, called Chirgwin, preaching to the text: "It is good for us to be here. Let us build three tabernacles", kept bending over to the right as he spoke, with his hands clasped, until we feared he would surely fall to the ground. Another would be so carried away in his ardour that the tears would stream down his face.

My own uncles preached at times, but, strangely enough, I do not remember ever attending their services. Names escape me, but I do remember some others — Matthews of Kerris, Roach, Cocks, and especially Richard Leah Pearce, of Newlyn, whose sermons were usually of a high order.

I think often of that Chapel, although it is a long time ago since I attended the services there. I can still hear my uncle in the back seats behind us, singing the Lord's Prayer in his sincere religious drawl; and a sharp tenor voice raised above all the others, somewhere in the middle range of pews to the right of us.

The Revival Services in the Chapel, in the evenings, stand vivid in my memory, all the more so, perhaps, since I attended them often as a wondering boy. I think really I should not have been there. It was not suitable for me. But there was an attraction about them — a sort of strange, emotional atmosphere invested them. It was in the nature of an entertainment for me as I sat.

The first Revivalist I remember in the Wesleyan Chapel was a Mr. Hunkin, father of a brilliant boy at Truro College, which I attended, who became later Bishop of Truro. After that came a very robust lady Revivalist, Miss Carkeek, who occupied the pulpit with real power, and whose persuasions brought many to the Communion Rail.

The emotion aroused at these meetings was extraordinary indeed. In the warmth of the Chapel it became more intense as the evening advanced, as specially chosen hymns exerted their hypnotic influence upon the congregation. As the most disturbing one of all for them was called for, the one which began: "Almost persuaded", the meeting reached its climax, and at the insistent appeal of the preacher, the call to "Come away", there would be desperate shufflings to the Communion Rail by many poor souls who had not done any real wrong. That hymn, "Almost persuaded", especially at that point in the evening, had been too much for them. It had wrought its disturbing work in the minds of many in that congregation, disturbance for good for some, and the words of King Agrippa were undoubtedly recalled to them: "Almost thou persuadest me to be a Christian".

Sometimes in these services some elderly bearded man would be on his feet, praying, quite eloquently, his supplications so intense that the tears would run down his face.

Once I heard a revivalist — I think it was Miss Carkeek — taking advantage of the high emotional state of her audience, make an unusual and special appeal: "Husbands, pray for your wives, wives for your husbands". It proved too much for a lady in one of the front pews, where she sat with her husband, Tom, a fisherman. "I pray for my husband," she cried, standing up, overwrought. It was a tense moment. Her husband, appalled at her outburst, resisted and kept his seat for a space, but finally uttered a "garm", a sort of desperate pained cry, rose up and lurched unsteadily to the Communion Rail.

I don't think the fisherman in question, or the lady his wife, could have done anything very wicked. In such an atmosphere as existed in the Chapel then it was not surprising that some quite excusable lapses of conduct could be magnified in the mind and become mortal sins.

Miss Carkeek, that formidable lady, was, I think, the most persuasive revivalist of all; but these meetings cannot be remembered with pleasure. There was something frightening about them. They played unfairly, I think on the emotions. Nevertheless, other revivalists were to follow Miss Carkeek, some who strove with high religious intent to influence those with whom they came into contact.

Next to the Chapel was the Vestry, an ample building where the Band of Hope meetings were held. My uncle, a staunch non-smoker and non-drinker, presided there at times, warning us about the evils of tobacco, its effects upon the human body. He showed us two hearts, one healthy and intact, the other diseased, hideous, showing the dire effects of the weed.

Heaven knows where he got the pictures from. And I think his warnings were a trifle exaggerated. I am rather frightened still, when I see that hideous heart in my imagination.

I have said that some of the old Wesleyans were narrow and bigoted. It was indeed so. The "Blessed Sabbath" could be for them, and their children, a sombre and unattractive day. Attendance at Chapel and Sunday School for the children was insisted on, and most normal and innocent week-day pleasures, such as fishing, swimming, picking apples even, were looked upon with great disfavour on that day. Even taking a walk was frowned upon. I remember my brother, quite a young man at the time, strolling in enjoyment on a lovely Sunday morning, being accosted by a very unhappy-looking man who had just come out of Chapel, and being asked the amazing question: "Don't you **believe** in God?" Such intolerance as that, though, was happily rare.

Let me not criticize too severely. Looking back, I think it was attractive to regard the Sunday as something special, to dress nicely, to see others nicely dressed, to be respectful in demeanour. There is much that is lost, nothing gained, in the careless observance of that special day, Sunday, that obtains today.

The narrowness of some of the Wesleyans will be apparent to my readers in a short and somewhat amusing little account, which must conclude my story of the Wesleyan Methodist Chapel.

It was customary for many people in the village to use the communal bake-houses, to which they would take their prepared dinners, puddings, cakes, etc., to be baked; also bread. They had their own special mark for the latter. Ned Downing told me that his mother had her bread baked at Carey's bake-house at the bottom of Commercial Road, and that her special mark was an ivy-leaf, a real ivy-leaf, stuck on to the bread. The bake-houses, some of them — I think the one at the Keigwin Arms especially — were used also on Sundays. Worshippers coming out of the Chapel on Sunday would often meet and mingle with the people emerging from the bake-houses with their Sunday dinners, all hot. This was regarded by the more bigoted Chapel-goers as an unfortunate and degrading encounter on the Sabbath. They could not very well alter their moment of exit from the Chapel. The sermon might be long; it might be short. There might be a Prayer-Meeting to prolong the session. But they did try to alter the time of exit from the bake-houses, to make it earlier. That must have been difficult. I am not sure if it ever succeeded.

One thing is certain, though. They did not object to their own dinners being cooked on the Sunday, or to their wives having prepared them beforehand. The Sunday dinner was sacrosanct. It had to be ready for them when they reached home.

XVI
The Ship Inn

It is March month. I am sitting by a blazing fire in the Ship Inn at Mousehole. There is a nasty east wind outside, but in here it is warm and comfortable. I have my glass of smuggler's ale before me, and I begin to think about my book, to wonder how on earth I shall be able to complete it. It seems to occupy my thoughts too much. If only that London chap hadn't been so persistent, egging me on to do something for which I felt incapable, I should never have thought about it at all. I am getting older now, and the task seems more monstrous every day.

Mary Greenhaugh, the landlady, comes over for a moment to talk to me, and as she speaks I glance up at the picture of the "Solomon Browne", in rough seas, above me, painted by Jack Pender — the lifeboat in which her husband perished. And I wonder how, in a short space of time, things can change, dramatically, how disaster can suddenly strike.

The door is ajar over there on the granite steps at the back of the Inn, and a distinguished gentleman, Admiral of the Fleet, Sir Caspar John, now sadly afflicted, comes courageously through in his wheel-chair. I feel glad that in the long day he finds easement for a while, and feeling friends.

I have been at a loss to find interesting subject-matter for my book, enough to fill it up. I expect everyone who writes has that difficulty. Now, as I sit here, thinking about it, I realise suddenly that I could perhaps write something about this Inn that might prove of interest to my readers. And that I will try to do, for there are lots of things I remember myself, and lots that I have gained from others.

The "Ship" is the only old Inn left of several that stood, almost in living-memory, and of the many that existed in more rollicking times, in the back centuries, when Mousehole was a flourishing seaport, Newlyn a "lesser fishing-town", and Penzance a mere village; long before the crusading zeal of Wesley had had its impact upon the population of Cornwall.

Nettie Pender in her instructive book has mentioned four Inns — apart from the "Ship" — which can almost be remembered by the older people of the village: the "Keigwin Arms", the "Old Standard", the "Dolphin" and the "Fisherman".

I can almost remember the "Keigwin Arms" myself. As a boy I knew a gentleman who was formerly connected with the Inn. He was actually living in my present cottage then, here in Penolva. He was nicknamed "Alabama" — as a result, I imagine, of his sojourn in the States — and he seemed to have a permanent bead of moisture at the tip of his nose.

The lay-out of the "Ship" has changed somewhat since I was young. What is now the little central room was formerly the service bar, with barrels raised on gantries against the wall. They had been introduced into a cellar below through an entrance outside, and were hoisted up from there when needed. In fact, one can see even now the wooden roller in the ceiling over which a rope passed to hoist the barrels into the room.

The larger bar-room stood as it is today, but a solid wall separated it from the present serving room, which was a sort of parlour, a private room where, I remember, we used to change for football, and where business people could meet and complete their deals.

The far lounge was a good deal smaller than it is now, separated from a kitchen behind it.

The floor of the present bar-room, and the passage leading to the back of the Inn, is paved in flat granite slabs, very neatly, and this adds to the ancient appearance and atmosphere of the building. The granite is coarse-grained, showing quite a lot of felspar crystals. It seems to me coarser than the Sheffield and Lamorna granites. Some say that it came from the old pier that used to stretch out from the Ship Inn, the stones of which were used to build the New Pier, in 1868—1870. I have no doubt that this Inn stood a very long time indeed before that, and that the original floor was of earthen construction.

The landlord of the "Ship" when I was young was a Mr. Williams, known as "Cap'n John". He had been Captain of a mine somewhere in South Africa or America. He was a tall, gaunt man, as was his namesake, landlord Williams, of Paul Inn. But they were not related, as we used to think.

Cap'n John had a son, William, locally known as "Dinkshy", and a daughter, Ethel, a much respected teacher in the village. Dinkshy served in the first World War, in the Black Watch, and, I believe, had a very rough experience indeed. He was a blacksmith by trade, and worked with Jim Bodinar in his forge at the end of the Gurnick, just short of the Salt Ponds, on the sea side of the road, where the boys would take their iron hoops to be scarfed. In the evenings, and when not engaged in their work, Dinkshy and his sister would serve behind the bar.

Dinkshy was a curious character. He would get very drunk at times, especially when going for a trip to Penzance of a Saturday evening. I have often met him returning from "town", as we called Penzance, on such an evening, in Nicky Harvey's bus, the "Glenville". He liked to be "one of the boys", was never happier than when he was in sympathetic, especially sporting, company. He looked at me intently, with bleared eyes, one evening in the bus, told me that I ought to have my "county cap" for soccer (for which I was not really qualified), and informed me, vaguely, that he had been playing rugby at Camborne. "I was picked out of the scrum like a mackerel," he said. I am sure he had not been playing, or could have played, the game at all. He was mad on rugby, though. He always imagined himself in the game. It was a common sight to see him, just prior to a match, where chaps were playing about with the ball, leading a rush, with arms outstretched, curiously eager, but quite ineffectual in his movements. He was imagining himself in a furious forward attack.

As I have said, Dinkshy was happy among his pals, his boon companions. Coming home, of a Saturday night, his eyes agleam, in that warm bus of Nicky's, he would join very heartily indeed, as the bus approached Mousehole, in the singing of the good old favourite, "Nelly Deane". He was a very quiet, gentle chap, really; and yet, sometimes, late at night, serving behind his own bar, after "time", he would show small sign of inebriation, and deal very sharply indeed with customers who were too slow to leave. He would give them their marching orders, I have heard, in no uncertain terms, like a sergeant-major.

I suppose beer and other drinks were pretty cheap in those days, but I often wonder, considering the strong feeling there was against alcohol in many quarters, how there could have been customers enough to make the Inn pay its way.

Outside the "Ship", and in front of Joe Rowe's shop and bakery, which is now the dining-room of the Inn, there was usually a group of men strolling up and down. I remember Richard Richards ("Double Dick", often shortened to "Double"), father of Charlie, and grandfather of Trevelyan, the coxswain of the "Solomon Browne". I remember also Sam Harvey, Bruce Wright, Richard Treeve Harvey, Bill Thurban, Johnnie Harvey, Johnnie Halse, Willie Harry, and Joe Rowe himself.

It was an interesting gathering, and the conversation was typical of the small groups that could usually be seen on the Cliff. It was all good-humoured, in spite of the difference of opinion expressed. Willie Harry, staunch Labour man, very sincere, stepping forth and gesticulating, was listened to attentively, but with a sort of amused tolerance, by his companions, if he championed his cause too ardently — as, indeed, he had far more justification for doing in those days than he would have today.

There was a lot of chewing tobacco in those days among the fishermen and yachtsmen of the village. It was comforting to have a quid in your mouth in the long nights at sea, waiting for the haul. And, sitting in the stern, one could more easily get rid of the waste product in the water than when ashore. I remember quite well that the fishermen kept their "chaw tobacca" (the "aw" in "chaw" pronounced as the o in "chop") in little Players tobacco-tins. Half-an-inch cut off would last quite a time, and, unfortunately, spitting would be a frequent necessity.

One man, Sam, was an inveterate chewer. He had done a lot of steamboating and yachting in his days. He "spoke fine" — as we used to say in the village — in more correct English than most of his companions. I ventured to ask him one day — for I often liked to speak to Sam — how much he chewed in a week, and he answered, "I de chew four ounces a week, and that's a tidy chew." That's what he said. I could hardly believe it possible.

Another group, before my time, was outside that Inn one day. My great-uncle Tom was there, with others, including Joe Rowe's father. Uncle Tom was a good thrower, especially with a handy little thin stone which we called a "haling", and the others were challenging him to throw from the Inn over the coping on the South Pier. Uncle Tom used to tell us about it, among other things, when he visited us at Paul, on Sundays, bringing his grand-children, Dick and Mary, of whom he was very proud.

There was a custom for some of the villagers at that time to put an aspirate "h" before some words. Uncle Tom told us — referring to the coping — "I could throw hon to it, but not hover it."

At the time of the challenge some of those around him tried to dissuade him from throwing at all, pointing out that there were fishermen on the pier, and that they might be hit. At that stage — and here is the exquisite humour of the story as told to us by my uncle — Joe Rowe's father interpolated with, "I'll be responsible for that!" "Then," said Uncle Tom, "I hove." It was not the best of his throws, did not reach the coping, and struck one of the fishermen on the pier, who, said my uncle, "went down like a ling" — a fisherman's way of putting it, born of long experience and observation. I have no knowledge of the extent of that fisherman's injury; but the stone in the course of its trajectory must have lost some of its striking force, and I hope therefore that no serious harm resulted.

The back entrance to the Inn is now in frequent use. I am not sure if it existed years ago. It is not wide enough for vehicles, but horses might have passed through to stalls there once. Indeed, Harry Drew told me that he had dug up a horse-shoe there. Of course, horse-shoes can be found almost anywhere, so that doesn't prove that horses were really stabled there.

In concluding my account of the Ship Inn, shall I say that if one had wished to slip in unseen in the old days when a half-pint of ale could destroy a reputation, then that back alley-way could have proved useful indeed.

XVII
The Shops, and Susan Mary's

There were quite a number of shops in Mousehole when I was young. In fact, the number is a little surprising when one considers that there wasn't a great deal of money to spend.

There was Freddie Hockin's — opposite the Harbour Office under the clock, where we bought liquorice laces and ladders with our Saturday pennies; Liza Jane's — where Caslake's now is; Joe Rowe's — now the dining-room of the Ship Inn; Pomeroy's — opposite the Inn; Susan Mary's — next door; Albert Wallis's — to which Pomeroy's moved later; Morris Ladner's — just beyond the present Post Office; Eddy's — along St. Clement's Terrace, later removed to the bottom of Raginnis Hill. Some of these had bakeries attached, like Joe Rowe's and Susan Mary's.

In addition to these there were quite a few smaller establishments. Sophie, in the Millpool, sold mainly vegetables. Pastorella, in the house over the river on the other side of Regent Terrace, sold what we called "Black Man's Toffee", made from black Barbados sugar. Ada Oliver, in a small house opposite the present Wheel House, sold groceries and sweets. Rebbie Blewett had a small shop in the region of Fox's Lane.

The butcher's shop now occupied by Mr. Tripp, who succeeded Mr. Billy Kneebone, was formerly occupied by Mr. Ernest Ladner, brother of Morris Ladner.

Beare's, butcher in the market at Penzance, came, I think on Saturdays, to a ground-floor room in the Mill Pool, part of the house once occupied by Bert Dyer.

Susan Mary's shop had, perhaps, the biggest custom of all these. She was a close relation of my family, and my mother lodged with her for a time when she came as a young woman to teach in Mousehole School.

I went often to fetch groceries for my mother from this shop when I was very young. I sat patiently, and wonderingly, on the sort of orange-box with a lumpy cushion in one corner, for quite a time, until Susan Mary's mother — Aunt Susan, my grandfather's sister — would notice me and upbraid Susan Mary for keeping me waiting so long.

There were few distractions for the fisher-women in those days. They loved to gather together in the shops for a chat, and tended to tarry for a while after making their purchases, especially in the darker evenings, when the oil lamps cast a soft warm glow. Susan Mary's shop was, I think, their favourite meeting-place. They were picturesque in their Paisley shawls, which most of them wore, but many of them were poor. They had never had much. There had been glad moments for them over the years, especially when the fishing had been successful, but for most of the time they had experienced hardship and harsh deprivation, borne with great courage and Christian faith. The story of the lean years could be read in some of the older lined faces, as they spoke together in the old way, in a language not quite so refined as would now be spoken by their children and grandchildren — a language that I could quite easily revert to myself even now, though, if I wished.

Susan Mary sold groceries of all kinds. I remember especially a huge lump of butter from which she cut, and a big bladder of lard. We used to compare, in our childish amused fancy, certain bald heads of the village to that bladder of lard. And it was, indeed, a very apt comparison.

She also sold tobacco — twist tobacco, rolled up in a ball, like string. She would weigh this in her scales, and I can see her now breaking off a piece, or adding a litte, to get the correct weight. She must have sold quite a lot of that tobacco, in spite of the fact that smoking, or chewing, was regarded by many in the village as a great evil. I am not at all sure that Susan Mary herself, brought up in a strict Wesleyan circle, did not privately condemn the habit.

From the ceiling of her shop was suspended a round basket full of eggs. It seemed quite a good place for them to be in, quite safe. I think there must have been some means of lowering and raising the basket, but that I cannot remember.

When times were bad, and the fishing a failure, the shops would be very generous indeed in allowing for later settlements. Susan Mary's desk, I distinctly remember, was always a confused mass of papers — wrapping papers and bills hastily compiled. I feel that she kept no very strict record, and that some bills were never paid — couldn't be paid! I have been told by more than one that she must have been a benefactor to many families.

Her saffron cake was highly thought of in the village, and her loaves. Down a few steps from the shop was a bakery. I remember the long-handled shovels pushing into the ovens. I rather fancy my great-aunt Susan controlled things down there; and Susan Mary had one or two very faithful helpers over the years, especially Sarah Wright. I think too that Susan's brother, Harry, who lived with her, must have given considerable help down there when he was not engaged in fishing.

What now is an upstairs bar and lounge of the Lobster Pot, overlooking the harbour, was Susan Mary's sitting-room. It seemed, thrust out over the harbour, something like the wide bridge of a ship, with commanding views. Sometimes we went, with our parents, to tea there — nearly always of a Sunday, when the Wesleyan Minister for the day had been invited. It was always a magnificent meal, ample, with tartlets and jelly and cream. We were young; and, to be sure, sitting quite well-behaved at that big round table, with Sunday manners, we enjoyed that meal immensely.

In those days there was no electricity, no gas, no cars, no water laid on, and water had to be fetched from one of the many chutes — "shotes" as we called them — in the village. One such was Fox's Lane "shote", and upon occasion Susan Mary would ask me, or one of my brothers, to fetch a bucket of water for her from there. It was not to burden us. As I have said before, there was a lot of smoking and chewing going on, especially outside Joe Rowe's shop, and spitting was, I am afraid, a necessity at times. She was afraid that, if she asked a fisherman to undertake the task, he might spit into the bucket.

I must now leave Susan Mary's shop. It has been, even for me, a certain pleasure in recalling for my readers the little incidents there. There is something that I cannot forget, though, something that has stuck in my memory. It is illustrative of the hard times, the poverty that existed in the village when the boats had brought nothing home. In that shop I have heard, often, meagre orders given — just for a few groceries, perhaps. There would be very little money for the women in their purses. Then I would hear a final request: "Putt in aperd o'nicey, Miss Harvey." ("Put in a hap'orth of sweets"). That small luxury would be put into a little conical paper bag. I am sad always when I remember that final little order. It was all that could be afforded!

I have become increasingly conscious, as I write, that I have been telling of the past, of a time when established customs and ways of life were not subject to the ceaseless and rapid change which has characterized most of the last half-century. Of course, it was my purpose right at the start to do as I have done, to speak of the past. I doubt if I could be clever enough, in any case, to write a modern story, or that I could interest my readers if I did. I feel sure, though, that very many of them would be grateful for a backward look.

The rapidity of change in modern times is disturbing, unsettling. Some philosophers have thought that when, as the result of happy discoveries and inventions, the word has reached to a decisive step forward, it would be wise to call a halt, for a long period, to enjoy what benefits had been gained. It certainly does seem that in our time certain reasonable bounds have been over-stepped, to the detriment of all.

XVIII
The Cave and the Meadows. The Guides.

Half-way up Raginnis Hill at Mousehole, a little narrow road on the left leads ultimately to a cave which is usually referred to as "The Mousehole". I have thought sometimes that the name of that cave might have influenced the name of the village, especially because of the termination, "hole". I had to reject that idea, however, upon reading in Nettie George's book that in his studious researches the Rev. Lach-Syzrma, one-time vicar of St. Peter's Church, Newlyn, had read of a village named "Mose hole" in the Charter of Edward the First. That is indeed close to the modern spelling.

The termination "hole" has been associated with "hayle" meaning "river" in Old Cornish. Of course a river ran through the village — more than one, in fact. Nettie gives a reference which states that the proper name of the village was "Moeshayle' — that "Moes" might have been the same as "Mowes", Cornish for "Young Women", so that the river might have been called "Young Women's River", and that it could have influenced the name of the village.

The Vicar found also that in early years the village was called "Mosal".

One thing is suggested to me by these names: that the pronunciation of the name of our village has changed but little through the ages, that people have spoken of the village as "Mouzel", as we now say, with small deviations, through the centuries.

The village seems also to have been known to the Old Cornish, at some date which is rather obscure, as "Porthenys" — clearly meaning "Island Port". It is a most attractive, and very suitable, name, and I would like Mousehole to be "Porthenys" still; just as I wish that Paul village were called **Saint** Paul today

The little meadows bordering the lane leading to the Cave, some of which have now been incorporated into the gardens of newly-built houses, were extensively cultivated not so many years ago. The soil is extremely rich there, and hedges of shrubs — quick-growing fuchsias especially, escallonia, privet, etc., were skilfully planted to lessen the damaging effect of the south-east winds, which could blow up suddenly in the Spring, and last sometimes for two or three weeks. In those meadows flowers were cultivated — daffodils, solidors (soleil d'ors), Scilly Whites, violets, anemones, polyanthus, wallflowers and others, all destined ultimately for Covent Garden and other markets, "Up Country", as we say.

These meadows have changed ownership and been rented by various people over the years. I am acquainted with some families in Mousehole who still work assiduously in them. My own brother spent several years of his retirement working in some delightfully quiet and secluded meadows leading up to the top of Raginnis Hill, and became a successful grower.

The flowers he grew — anemones, violets, polyanthus and others — were beautiful there, and graced many a market, and many a sick bedroom and drawing-room later. But there was more in those meadows than the flowers and the intriguing delight of watching them grow, day by day. There was quiet. A pervading quiet. And sometimes a robin at one's feet. No-one had placed a machine of artificial noise there. The cacophany of jazz and of much modern music was absent. There was a Presence that disturbed

"With the joy of elevated thoughts"

in between the hedgerows there, and in the uncultivated spots, those

"Little lines of sportive wood run wild."

That Presence drew many, I think, in the past, to those lovely meadows, and, perhaps, still draws a few to some of the secluded spots.

My friend Douglas Hunter has spent many enjoyable moments since he retired to Mousehole in a lovely little plot lower down towards the Cave, growing, in his case, a few vegetables. On a summer day it can be hot, tropical, delightful down in those meadows. The work is hard, though, at times, especially when the soil has slipped downward over a long period, and has to be shovelled laboriously towards the top again. A Cornish shovel, a delightfully-pitched implement, sufficed for that in the old days, and avoided all the bending down necessitated in the use of the modern spade.

I believe the Pomeroy family of Mousehole tilled quite a few meadows on the left of the Cave lane, growing vegetables and flowers for their shop, and fruit trees. I am sure they grew blackcurrants.

One day in London, walking in Earl's Court, I was pleased to discover, in a florist's shop there, some lovely Cornish violets with a Mousehole name on the tag: "W. Harvey". He worked some of the larger meadows towards what we call "The Crackers"; as he still does, I believe. The Torrie family still work some meadows, too, and my close acquaintance, Edgar Wallis.

I must not forget to say that early potatoes were also grown in the Cave meadows. I remember a potato that was highly thought of, but rarely seen now, and extensively grown — "Sharp's Express", which some of my readers will surely remember.

On a Saturday sometimes, as a boy, after the potatoes had been "drawn", I would be down in one of those hot meadows picking up potatoes that had been left in the ground, for a farmer who lived in the village. And for that work I was proud to earn sixpence. It was enough to buy a good pocket-knife from the Stores.

Speaking generally of these meadows, I have to say, regretfully, that most of them are now badly overgrown.

I walked through the lane to the Cave only a few days ago. It was a longer walk than I had expected, and, towards the end, damp and steep, offering no safe foothold on the sloping and irregularly-planted stones. However, helped by clutching at outstanding branches of the shrubs on either side, I was able to overcome the awkward descent, and to emerge, quite abruptly, on to a delightful grassy level, on the top of the cliffs, where, after the daring Spanish raid of 1595, cannons had been mounted to deal with any future rash intrusions of the armed galleons. The cannons are no longer there, having been removed a long time ago.

This grassy level and the flat granite stones nearby was a little area we called the Battery, a much favoured spot, where visitors would hesitate for a pleasurable moment before attempting the difficult descent to the Cave. In former days one could buy soft drinks there from a stall which had been erected by one of the villagers.

But why do I speak of these things when one is here in the midst of a startling array of giant cathedral-like granite rocks. Down there the sea laps against them as they rear up, more massive than I would ever have imagined. They are dignified and grand — a foretaste, a promise, of the great cliffs further west.

There is a huge granite rock, a small island at high tide, just offshore. It is the Merlin Rock. That name, and the hollow whispers from the Cave, as yet unseen, cast their spell. And suddenly it is all in the past, ages ago, aeons ago. They were there, the shining rocks, They **are** there. They will **always** be there. The story they tell us is of wondrous things, the same things that are told by the great cliffs of Penwith, further west into the magic land.

The descent to the Cave, over the huge granite rocks, is difficult, and must be entered upon with care. There were rails at some narrow and dangerous points, and, I think, iron brackets for holding on to still exist.

The cavern itself was probably an adit, a sea entrance — like Dicky Daniel's Hole on the other side of the village — leading to a "Bal", or mine. This particular bal has now been filled up with overburden from the greenstone quarries at Newlyn. Quite a sensation it was in our young days to look down into the deep, sinister depression, from the top of Raginnis Hill. There was danger there too, for the protecting rails were almost on the verge. The road itself caved in just there some years ago, and had to be carefully reconstructed.

My wife played around this spot as a girl. She lived in the farm up above — Raginnis Farm. She says that according to tradition the bal was a copper mine; that in the farm-house then there were specimens of copper ore that had come from it originally, and been preserved. Before the bal was filled in, she says, the sides were very attractive, with ferns growing, and all sorts of grasses, flowers, bluebells etc., even elder bushes.

If one goes down through the "Bal Gate", as it has always been called, protecting rails can be seen on the right, along the sides of the hollow as it deepens. This is a lovely, twisting way to the rocks and the Cave, through the little meadows, some of which are cultivated still.

It has been suggested that the land in this Cave area, especially in its higher reaches towards Raginnis, was once the property of the Newlyn Quarries, and that it was purchased or rented later by farmers and others for cultivation. I doubt if that can now be proved. They would be searching for stone, probably. And the existence of certain small long-abandoned, overgrown quarries off the road and in the vicinity does suggest that there might have been some serious exploratory diggings in the past.

I have spoken of the ferns growing in the sides of the Bal before it was filled in. Ferns, and some quite beautiful ones, grew also in the Cave itself; and behind them, and in the frequent hollows high up, jackdaws built their nests. Sometimes their young, fully fledged, would fall from the nests, and as boys we rescued them, and they became pets for us, much loved pets. It was quite a common sight in the village to see boys with friendly jackdaws on their shoulders. I always had one myself. They would call to you happily if you spoke to them and at the same time tilted up their beaks. It was the habit to clip their wings early on to prevent them from taking to the air and escaping. But later I think they had no wish at all to escape.

I cannot say much more about this Cave, this "Mousehole". It is impressive, seen from the rocks on the shore, and still a great attraction to visitors in the Summer months.

The so-called "guides" who assisted them were quite well-known to me when I was young. They would get into conversation with the visitors and persuade them to visit the Cave — painted by them in rather extravagant colours — under their guidance. I don't think any fixed fee was ever demanded for the service, though the task was by no means an easy one, and took a considerable time. Sometimes quite small sums were given to them. There were occasions when, playfully and very unfairly, even wickedly, deceit was practised. A man once dressed up as an attractive woman, and, at the conclusion of the accompanied trip, rewarded the guide with a very small sum indeed. A penny, I think.

These guides were criticized, looked down upon by some of the villagers as lazy scroungers. I am not at all sure that such criticism was justified.

The men were not fishermen, most of them. They did not seem to have any fixed employment. They were certainly very poor; so poor that when I think of them now I feel sad, and wonder how on earth they managed at all. Not everybody was naturally equipped for a fisherman's life then. Indeed, to some it must have been a frightening prospect. And other jobs were extremely rare. Most of my own relations, young men, had to strike out bravely for themselves, emigrate to South Africa, to America, Australia, New Zealand. I cannot really think of these guides as just lazy men.

They had considerable ability. They could converse well, intelligently; had good powers of description, were quite efficient in the particular work in which they were engaged.

Competition was severe among them, and the less robust were apt to be overawed and frightened by the stronger men. Such a condition might last for years, reaching to an unbearable stage, when matters would reach a crisis.

I have a vivid memory of seeing two guides — not young men either — in desperate conflict, in front of Joe Rowe's shop, on the Cliff. They had been fighting for some time, had both fallen in fatigue, and were now flat on the ground, prone, worn out, closed fists punching at targets no longer clearly defined, meeting only the surrounding air.

One of them rose, tiredly, to his feet at last — one who had been considered the weaker, a man not at all aggressive by nature. He spoke, addressing the crowd who had not even attempted to intervene. I can hear him saying now — I was just a boy, appalled at the violence — "I ben afraid o' that man all my life, but I aren't afraid ob'm any more." He had - had, if anything, the better of the struggle. From thenceforth he could be a guide fearing nobody, a different man, himself.

The police intervened at the end of that bitter fight, and the two men had to appear in court at Penzance. They were each fined £5.

I think I can conclude my story of the guides, and perhaps amuse my readers by giving the reaction of the more violent of the two men to that decision of the Penzance magistrates: "I fought for King and Country," he said, "for five bloody years. I fight for myself for five minutes and I am fined five bloody pounds!"

XIX
The Shoemakers

There are now no shoemakers in the village, But when I was a boy there were several. First of all, there was Willie Jeffery's. He had a little not-so-easy-to-find place at the bottom of Brook Street, just behind his house facing the Lobster Pot. You went through a little entrance, now closed by a door, and then into a workshop on the left. This workshop looked onto an inner yard. There would Willie be, sitting on his stool, chewing, or with a quantity of sprigs in his mouth.

It was a cosy little place, and it was the custom, especially in the winter, for fishermen pals of his, many of them, when the weather was bad and the fishing slack, to sit around the warm stove and chat together. There were also quite long periods of silence, broken only by the entrance of new customers.

Willie himself was slightly lame. He was a rather reticent person. He never spoke a lot, and when he did, it was in a curious high, piping voice. I have taken shoes down to him many times to be repaired. He would take them without much to say, examine them carefully — he was an excellent workman — and then lay them aside, with just a remark as to when I could get them back. That was usually in a very short time.

His brother Charlie was a shoemaker too. I am not sure, but I think he worked with his brother earlier on, but finally had his own workshop, and lived up the steps on the left in Fore Street, just below the old Stores, where my great-uncle Tom and his wife Mary lived. That was a long time ago. I didn't see my aunt Mary often. She was a quiet soul, poor, a good manager with the little she had, delighted to see us when we called. It was a cosy little place to step into, typical of so many of the fishermen's cottages in those days, the atmosphere a little close upon entering, with a coal fire in the grate. I look back over the years to a sort of attractive homeliness that is difficult to describe.

Willie Jeffery's business was continued by his son, Wilfrid, one of my Mousehole friends, who died quite recently.

The Harvey family had an extensive business in shoemaking at that time too. They worked all together, William, Nicky, Chris, three brothers, and their father Philip, in a building quite close to the North Pier in Mousehole. There is a little alley-way beside the present gift-shop called "The Mouse Hole". You went towards the end of that, up a little slope, and found yourself in a fair-sized meadow. Here was their workshop, the family Harvey. The smell of leather and waxed thread was strong in your nostrils as you entered. Of course, all the work was in leather in those days. They made hob-nailed boots, which were extensively worn then, especially by the boys. They supplied the fishermen with boots suitable to their trade — thigh boots, half-boots especially; even the youngsters often wore half-boots, because they were engaged, many of them, in helping in the boats at an early age. They wore their half-boots to school frequently, having had no time to change from their fishing gear.

The Harveys, like the Jefferys, were expert workmen. As time went on, and rubber sea-boots became available, the character of their work changed, of necessity, and they became virtually cobblers, engaged mainly in repair-work.

The meadow where they worked was owned by Freddie Hockin, the shopkeeper in the village, and was bought later from Walford Hockin, his son, by Arthur Richards, an elderly fisherman friend of mine who lives in his cottage on the Bank.

Arthur will be going down to his little punt alongside the North Pier, now that the baulks in the harbour mouth are up. It is interesting to see him in the quaint and practical old gear which he has not abandoned — cap, guernsey, heavy serge trousers, half-boots — which now, I think, must be of rubber. He is eighty-eight, two years older than I am. He will get into his punt, unmoor her skilfully, stand up in the stern, and scull her out to bait crab-pots, somewhere out "'tween isle and shore". All the experience of the past is with him. There is no hurried movement. You would expect him to sit. No, he stands up in the little punt, casts a look at the weather, ships his oar over the stern, sculls quietly — one-handed, left-handed often, facing "forrard", until he reaches his markers, the buoys. He pulls up the pots, baits them. I think he tends them for somebody else. He has a little outboard motor over the stern to use in emergency. He doesn't seem to tire at the sculling at all, and, I am sure, enjoys himself out there.

Arthur has two cottages on the Bank. Over the porch of the one he lives in he has painted a little craft and her name, "La Mouette", the French word for "sea-gull". It is rather a lovely name for a fishing-boat. She wasn't very big — only about eighteen feet long — and he bought her at Mousehole, when he had more or less retired from serious fishing. She came originally from Coverack.

Also over that porch Arthur has painted a fishing-boat of his, "The Golden Sunset", P.Z. 178, and over the door of the other cottage is a painting of the "Two Boys", with her name — another of his boats.

Arthur took me up some narrow stone steps beside his house to the meadow of which I have spoken, where the Harveys cut and hammered and stitched, the meadow which he bought from Walford Hockin. His memory is good. "Up there in the corner," he said, "was a stable where Nicky kept his mare, "Polly"; and down there in the lower corner was a shed where Milly, Nicky's sister, did her washing."

Arthur had a little garden up there. There was a lot of blue elvan about, especially one very large boulder which he called the "Logan Rock". It moved at a push, like the more famous one towards Land's End, in the old days before it became almost obscured by wild growth.

Quite a mass of blue elvan rock (greenstone) is conspicuous in front of his two cottages, at their base, and, indeed, in their immediate surroundings. It was all a part, as Arthur said, of the formation we called "Carn Topna".

I knocked on Arthur's door one evening, and found him in his cosy back-kitchen, reading the paper. Above him was a little budgerigar in a cage, quite free to come out at will. Good company for him, I thought. I said, "You're fond of that bird, Arthur?" He smiled. "That's life," he said. I liked that reply. Arthur is unmarried. That bird above him twitters happily. It is a delightful companionship.

The Harvey family lived formerly in the house on the left as you go into the barking vats. There they ran a Post Office. Nicholas distributed the letters, and rode with them on his mare "Polly" into the country. I can remember him well, riding up the lane towards Paul. Later, his family moved to the house named "Zuriel", recently a restaurant and gift shop, which was once an old cottage close to what was known as Sampy's Corner. There they still ran the Post Office, and sold boots and shoes.

Nicky — as we always called him — and his brother Chris were very smart cyclists. They raced often on the St. Clare ground at Penzance on August Bank Holidays, against opponents from as far away as Plymouth. I am not quite sure, to this day, which of the two was the faster cyclist. Chris was an extremely venturous young man, engaged at times in quite perilous enterprises. I remember that one day he rode from the New Pier to the Old Pier, over the baulks, on his bike — a quite daring performance. He was very inventive. He attached some contrivance cleverly to his bike once, and attempted to cycle to the Island; but I think that attempt was a failure. He is said to have ridden along the top of the wall bordering Penzance Station — where you look dizzily down from it on to platform one. That gives me a shudder still. I think he must have been secured in some way to prevent a terrible fall.

Nicky went to America in 1913, I think to Glenville, and stayed for several years. Upon his return he was enterprising enough to buy a bus, called the "Glenville", which ran between Mousehole and Penzance, for a fare of tenpence return. It was a "Dodge", I think. No doubt, Nicky was well acquainted with that noted American firm. Its seats ran lengthways, down the sides of the bus. If not the first, it was certainly almost the first bus ever to be seen in the village, and constituted the beginning of a most efficient and moderately-priced service along the same route now run by Nicky's two sons. They have several buses now, along with others, on the road to Penzance.

I think I have already spoken of the old "Glenville" bearing its passengers home of a Saturday evening, late, from Penzance. One night the young Welsh poet, Dylan Thomas, was making that journey home — to the "Lobster Pot", I think, in company with his boon companions. I saw him get out, unsteadily, at Mousehole, under the clock. "That's Dylan Thomas," Dorothy, my wife's cousin, told me. It was the first time I had ever seen him. Dylan was drunk. He reeled as he made for Joe Rowe's and the "Lobster Pott". Unsure of his direction, he lurched into the harbour rails there, and, happily, they brought him up. Someone must have helped him then to his room, but I have no recollection of that. Dylan could so easily have been one of the harbour casualties of which I have spoken earlier.

I have often wondered what thing it was in that young man's life, in the experience of that young inspired poet of the felicitous phrase, what crashing of ideals, what shattering disturbance, perhaps, of his exalted view of woman, what appalled dismay at the realisation of his own shortcomings, his own inadequacy, could have led him to a sort of hazy comfort, an unsatisfying oblivion, in drink. It was sad for him. But he is not alone. There are so many of great promise who have travelled the same road — leaving us, fortunately, with some jewels of great price, nevertheless.

There were two other shoemakers that I remember, vaguely, in the village. One was my friend Herbert Victor's father. I cannot recall now where his workshop was, but I think it was in an extension of the house called the "Wheel House", opposite the entrance to the Millpool. The other was a man with a club foot, called Clemo. He had a little place opposite the Ship Inn, entered by a door just on top of the stone steps leading down to the harbour there. I am not sure if the door is still there, for the place has been altered quite a lot in recent years. Clemo, like the other shoemakers, worked in leather, and made, like them, thigh boots and half-boots for the fishermen.

XX
The Barbers' Shops

As a boy in the village at the beginning of the century I well remember Barber Quick, commonly known as "Timmy Noggy". It is strange that we never knew — indeed I doubt if many adults ever knew either — how that curious nickname came about. Some years ago now I came across the unusual word "timenoguy" in a modern dictionary. It signified "a rope stretched from place to place in a ship, especially one to prevent the foresheet fouling", and I realised, all the more so since "Timmy Noggy" and "timenoguy" were almost identical in pronunciation, that here was the solution of the mystery. Barber Quick must have served on a ship at some time or other, and in conversation must have used the word more frequently than was good for his respectable standing. It is astonishing how apt the villagers of that time were to assign nicknames, how easily Richard Richards could become "Double Dick", and how the nickname would stick for ever afterwards. I knew a man who was a great fan of the Plymouth Argyle football team of those days. His enthusiasm led him to refer so often to that team, so often to include the name in his conversation, that he was referred to, in fun, as "Plymouth Argyle". The same gentleman, unfortunately, introduced his statements so often with the two words, "As regards", that others, somewhat wickedly, and even in his presence, would preface what they had to say with the same two words.

Barber Quick had his shop in a room under the clock at Mousehole, next to the Harbour Office. It must have been hard work for him there, for the room was often full of fishermen awaiting their turn for a shave or haircut — smokers, chewers, non-smokers — too many, one would have thought, for one man to deal with. And, of course, there would be boys there too, anxiously waiting.

The man being shaved would have a sheet of paper on his shoulder, upon which would be spread, as the shaving proceeded, lather from the razor mixed with hair from the cut beard. The smell of this, of the tobacco, the spent quids in the spittoons on the sanded floor, the cut hair lying everywhere, rose to the nostrils in the close atmosphere, in that small room with the window permanently shut. As a boy there, waiting my turn for a haircut, I am not at all sure that the smell of it was wholly objectionable to me. There was warmth, a certain cosiness, a curious interest in the company of the fishermen, most of whom I knew well. I would, however, be restless, in a state of apprehension, for Barber Quick was a bit rough with his clippers sometimes, and the consequent tweaks at the back of a boy's neck could be feared, and painful, indeed, in prospect.

I forget, of course, how much one had to pay for the shaving or the haircutting, but it was certainly a very small sum.

Barber Quick had his relaxing moments. He was a keen fisherman, and loved to anchor his little boat just behind the North Pier, and fish for bass. I don't know what bait he used, whether it was pilchard, or mackerel, or slugs dug from the harbour mud. But he was obviously very knowledgeable as to the habits of that particular fish, and would know what bait to use. Whether he was very successful in his fishing I do not know. I think he must have been, otherwise he would surely not have anchored so often in that particular spot. I am inclined to think that he took a pleasure in being out there in his small boat, in any case; that he liked the quiet, the solitude; that, indeed, the fishing was for him a secondary pleasure.

In the year 1910, another barber, Richard Ladner, who had learnt his trade with Cecil Gilbert at Newlyn, set up his hairdressing and shaving shop at Mousehole, on the site of the present paper-shop on the Cliff. It was practically a new building, and had been erected where two small cottages formerly stood. I remember the cottages quite well. They faced towards the west rather than towards the south, in what we called the "Ope". A family called Worth lived in one of them. Most of the native residents of the village will remember "Tommer" Worth, a fisherman.

Richard Ladner died in 1963, and his business was continued for a few years by his son, Owen. By that time the rather small saloon, entered immediately from the Cliff, had been considerably enlarged, with a view to a more extensive business, and the saloon itself transferred to an adjacent back room.

I have no personal knowledge of another barber's shop which must have existed somewhere opposite the Ship Inn. In the year 1837 a quay was constructed, and ran out from there. It lasted until 1868, when it was demolished, and the stones used to help build the present North Pier. Owen Ladner told me that my uncle Edwin, my father's brother, who lived to be over a hundred, had once related to him that, as a boy, he had stood upon that old quay, in a queue, waiting to have a hair-cut. So that, as I have said, there must have been a barber's shop somewhere at the end of that quay. It was perhaps where Joe Sleeman's house stood, close to Susan Mary's shop. At any rate, that is what Owen Ladner told me that my uncle had said.

It is strange how often that little area round Joe Rowe's and Susan Mary's and the Ship Inn has had a place in my story. And stranger still when I suddenly recollect that Phil Cattran, a young Mousehole man, had a barber's shop there. I can see his pole now, outside a house with a porch, just between the Inn and Brook Street. Phil lived with his family, when a boy, at Brook Villa, opposite the Old School. John Birch, the headmaster, often went across there for his lunch after morning school. We used to buy lovely apples there, too. I don't think Phil carried on the business for long. He finally left for the States, and was succeeded in the house by Joe Warren and his wife, who sold ice cream and soft drinks. Later, George Pomeroy and his wife sold fish and chips there. The fish and chips were good, too. I have never tasted better. The shop was very busy indeed most evenings. The Pomeroys had previously engaged in the same business where the old post-office used to be, at the entrance to the bark-house, on the left.

There may have been other barbers' shops in the village in the beginning of the century, but I can only remember the ones of which I have spoken.

XXI
Books

As Nettie Pender says in her little book, there was a Book Club in the village, formed in the early years of last century, and flourishing from that time onwards. There was also a Mousehole Reading Society. Nettie gives a list of over twenty members of that Society — an interesting list, for the names are almost all of Mousehole families.

I think what she calls "a great thirst for knowledge" had always existed in the village, strengthened perhaps by Methodism and the religious impact of John Wesley, who first came to Mousehole in 1766.

It is interesting to note, as Nettie records, that the books selected for the Book Club were all of solid intellectual worth — works of History, Biography and Philosophy mainly.

There was also a Tract Society. I well remember the tracts being handed in regularly at our home in Mousehole. They consisted of just a few pages, wrapped in brown paper; simple little accounts of religious experiences; tales of personal encounters with the Devil in all its forms, such as drunkenness or immorality, and final redemption; stories of the sea, of the lifeboat, of the saving of souls. They were distributed by ladies enthusiastic for the Methodist cause, each lady having her special round. It was all done in simple faith, and worthy of remembrance because of that.

At school on Friday mornings, I remember, just before lessons began, we all stood in groups, boys and girls, round Mr. Birch's desk in the schoolroom. It was the time for reading what we called "Acts of kindness". A boy or girl would have the courage to stand up before the others and read some moving story, in content similar to those I have told about in the Tracts. Is it a small thing to record? I think not. A wise headmaster had given a high place to poetry in that school, as I have already told, conscious as he was of its refining influence; and I think he visualised in these readings the same happy result.

I have striven, unsuccessfully so far, to find out if it were possible for those outside the Borough of Penzance to borrow from the Free Library in the Morrab Road, Penzance, which was established in 1894, and at first, I think, available only to the rate-payers and business people of that town. That Library has recently, with the superb Reference Library in its upper room, become one of the finest in south-west Britain. It is not certain if it was entirely free early in the century, even to the residents of the Borough. My Mousehole friend, Mc. Fadyean, who, with his brother, attended the County School (the present Humphrey Davy Grammar School) with me at the opening in 1910, seems to remember that the Penzance subscribers paid twopence to borrow a book there. Mac was a Penzance boy, and, sad to say, he lost his brother in the first World War.

Others suggest that outside the Borough it was possible at that time to borrow if one held what was called a "Visitor's Card".

I wish I knew more about the possibility of borrowing at that Library at that time, especially for the people of the surrounding district. But I have found it difficult to make the necessary contacts. Even the present Staff of the Library cannot assist me in the matter.

Of course, when the Borough was extended during my father's term of office as Mayor, in 1934, and the villages of Mousehole, Newlyn, Paul, Heamoor and Gulval were incorporated, the Free Library was then really free to all in the extended area.

I believe that anyone, even those outside the Borough, could always become subscribers to the superb Morrab Gardens Library, founded in 1818, for a payment, originally, of one guinea. It surprised me, when reading in Cyril Noall's book, "The Penzance Library", that that annual subscription had lasted until the year 1946, when it was decided to increase it to the still small figure of £1.10s., that being the first increase since the Library was founded.

Bridger's, formerly in Market Jew Street, opposite Barclay's Bank, had an important small lending library. I remember borrowing books there for my mother when I was a young man. I think also that one could borrow from Boots.

There were few conveyances early on in the century, and I think borrowings from these sources, as far as the country people were concerned, were comparatively rare. I know that my mother used to walk to Penzance and back, six miles, to change her books at Bridger's. There were many excellent volumes on Mr. Bridger's shelves, too.

Some Mousehole people bought books for themselves, and exchanges were frequent. We exchanged with Mrs. Kelynack, Teare's mother, who lived in what as boys we called Jimmy Brookham's Street, the one leading down over the steps from the Millpool towards the harbour. Jimmy, like Teare, was one of my boyhood friends. I remember his mother well, but not his father. I am not quite sure that I have spelt his surname correctly. Theirs was the first cottage on the left going down that street, a humble little place, with small windows to keep out the wind, typical of so many of the cottages in Mousehole at that time. They were poor, mother and son, and it was dark inside, with only the barest necessity of furniture. The big cellar next door, where, undoubtedly, in the earlier days, much work connected with the fishery had been carried on, must have proved useful to them. I don't know what change it has undergone. Jimmy went to the States, and I have never met him since those young days.

The Kelynack family were great readers. Teare told me that he would walk to Penzance with his uncle some days to purchase books — I think at a shop at the bottom of the Arcade, in Market Jew Street.

There was a Mrs. Rickett, too, with whom my mother exchanged books.

How wonderful it was then to be introduced to a book such as "The Mill on the Floss", to remember it ever after; to talk of the great books of last century round our kitchen table!

Richard Ladner, in addition to his barber's business, sold newspapers and periodicals, and had a small lending library. His son Owen continued the lending business after his father's death in 1963, but closed the library shortly after. I remember that the borrowing price for the books had been twopence. He increased his newspaper business by acquiring a round for Sunday newspapers, which had formerly been supplied by roundsmen from Penzance.

His shop has become a very important one, thronged with visitors in the Summer season. In addition to the magazines and periodicals, papers, stationery of all kinds, and tobacco, there are important books for sale there, especially those based upon the locality and dealing with the life and history of the Cornish villages.

Available, of course, to those who could afford them in those early days, were the daily papers, such as the "Daily News" and the "Daily Chronicle" (which two merged later to become the "News Chronicle"), the "Times", the "Morning Post", the "Daily Express", the "Daily Mirror", the "Daily Sketch", and others, which, like those I have listed above, had persisted for a very long time.

Great favourites for local news were the "Cornishman" and the "Evening Tidings". I can still hear the shrill tones of the little woman selling editions of the latter in the streets of Penzance on a Saturday night, and her repeated cry. I will scan it for you as she sang it: "Evening Tidings! Evening Tidings!" One heard it in the far streets as she continued her round. It was like a song. I hope that the paper made it worth her while, for she seemed rather frail, and the nights were often chilly and wet.

I remember the "Methodist Times" and the "Sunday Companion". In the latter were stories, serials, by the Cornish brothers, Joseph and Silas Hocking.

My mother always took "John O'London's Weekly" — an interesting literary publication, and the "Review of Reviews", which had been founded by W.T. Stead, the noted spiritualist, whose views upon religion and politics were freshly independent, if somewhat puzzling at times, and who perished in the terrible Titanic disaster, in 1912.

XXII
Model Luggers. Regattas. Magic Coves.

Many boys in the village, as might be expected, were fond of constructing their own little model luggers. A block of wood, seasoned, dry, was easy to obtain in those early days, and the expertise displayed in making the small craft was truly remarkable. Of course, the boys had good sharp pocket-knives, obtained at the village stores for sixpence, and had been chipping and cutting pieces of wood from childhood.

They bent to their work in these constructions with a knowledge and love of the luggers acquired over the years. I made some of them myself, not very good ones, I am afraid. The work was difficult, and looking back I wonder how it could have been done at all. In our cellars we shaped the boat, made the masts, the sails, the yards, the rudder. I remember, vaguely, certain operations that must have been very difficult — the attaching of the keel, for instance. We had some lead usually, and we melted it somehow or other. I have a vague remembrance of sand used in making a lead mould of the keel; of tin-tacks attached to the bottom of the boat to make it secure. It must have been difficult, but I am sure we did not think so then. We did it, easily. There was a certain amount of gouging out to be done, and, strangely enough, I think we used the round end of a pen-nib, fixed firmly in something, to achieve that. Amazing! I cannot recall how it was done. But the little lugger, suitably painted, would ultimately appear, complete with foresail, mizzen, and perhaps topsail over the latter.

We would push the little craft off from the harbour steps, or from some accompanying punt, at full tide, fix the rudder so that she might follow a straight course, and watch her progress, hopefully. A boy, his head slightly inclined, would follow her along her course, closely, his half-cupped palm extended and moving in concert with her increasing speed. It was a serious, critical affair, that first test. The rudder might have to be adjusted later, the sheets let out more, or less — all the little operations that, with accumulated experience, could easily be carried out.

Sometimes larger, more ambitious models would be taken out, accompanied by punts, to try their paces in wider and more troubled waters "'tween isle and shore". They would not all be lugger-rigged either, for some of our fishermen had been yachting from time to time, and, proud of the craft in which they had served, had models of them in their homes. Needless to say, these models were beautiful and looked upon with envious eyes by the youngsters. They would be difficult to overtake too, in their trials, especially if there was a tidy breeze blowing.

"I think I'll be a sailor." Picture by Walter Langley

In the Regattas, held once a year in Mount's Bay, with the Low Lee Buoy as one of the markers, the sailing qualities of the real luggers, big and small, and the expertise of their crews, would be adjudged by keen watchers at strategic points along the shore or on the rising land beyond Mousehole Quarry, which we always referred to as Klondyke.

There would be feverish excitement ashore on these occasions, especially if there were a stiff breeze in the bay. Anything might happen. For the luggers were fast sailers, and in the heeling boats at high speed there could be danger — in tacking, in changing of sails, in the hectic shifting of ballast (iron half-hundredweights), in rounding the buoys. The movements aboard had to be rapid and effective, and the danger of collision was never absent. A mast might be "carried away", a sail torn to ribbons. There were moments, if you like, of unfairness, when a lugger would take the wind of another, deliberately, and so change the course of events. But I cannot go too seriously into these happenings. It was all in the accepted strategy of the game.

One thing is certain: that these regattas were happy diversions in the life of the village, and the subject, later, for expert comment and criticism.

I should have mentioned at the outset, of course, that the luggers of Mount's Bay would be competing in these events — those from Mousehole, Newlyn and Porthleven, and perhaps some from St. Ives too. Local rivalries were strong, and the excitement therefore all the more intense.

I have some short extracts from my uncle's diary which have interested me specially, because the lugger mentioned — the "Temperance Star" — belonged to my family:

"**July 30th 1892.** The Regatta was held. Thos. Matthews's seine-boat secured first prize, namely Silver Cup".

"Temperance Star" 1st prize (Cup & £4). The Channel Fleet has been in the Bay during this week. Searchlights were shown with great splendour."

"**June 2nd 1895.** "Temperance Star" brought in 3 Burn of hakes, which were taken to Newlyn, and brought exceptionally high price — 36/9d. per Burn."

The "Temperance Star", P.Z. 427, was registered in 1889, and sold in 1900. (Information supplied to me by my friend Wilfrid Pender).

I felt, at a given moment, that some of my writing had become matter-of-fact, rather dull. So, on this lovely morning, Thursday, May 26th, which happened to be the first really warm and sunny day of a miserable year, so far, I went over the rocks on the north side of the village as far as Penlee Point. I had not been there for a long time. I wanted to recapture something of the past, to revisit "past scenes of delight", to see if the magic of those rocks, those shining pebble beaches, was upon them still; hoping, too, that if it were indeed so, some of that magic might enter into my story, as I believe it must have done when I was dreaming of the beautiful luggers.

It has been noted by many writers that on the south side of the Old Harbour Pier the rock formation, right up the coast to Lamorna and beyond, is of granite — in some places lovely clean, smooth granite, rearing to massive proportions at times. On the north side of the harbour the formation is of greenstone, which in Cornwall is called "blue elvan". As boys, for some reason, we did not go far along the granite rocks on the southern side, although, of course, we were well acquainted with the Mousehole Cave and the impressive formation there, reached by a different route, a little way inland.

On the north side there is, first, a pebble beach where ladies put out their washing in the old days, and the fishermen hung their hake and cod and ling upon supports to dry.

The next beach, round the corner where the glorious Mount comes into view, and the inner stretches of the bay, is composed, like the former, of pebbles, shining like jewels, some of them, when the flowing tide comes lapping over them. It was there that, as boys, we came to swim, several times a day. The weather seemed more settled and warmer then, and the rocks were sometimes too hot to lie upon.

This cove, called "Tavis Vor", gave its name to the present guest-house just above. My father built it in 1919. I designed it. I named it. We lived there many years. I laid out a little garden there, with granite steps leading up to it, for my mother, which has since, under the pressure of the times, been demolished to make a space for the modern engines to park. I built a little bird-bath there too, of small granite stones. I built it lovingly, for the same garden plot. I ought not to have let it go when "Tavis Vor" was sold, but I was away at the time, and could not say that it was mine, not for sale. However, it was legitimately sold. But I fancy that "Tavis Vor" is mine still, and that that little bird-bath, now in someone else's garden, is mine also, always will be mine.

I built another bird-bath, much later, for my brother. I treasure that; but the first little bird-bath I treasure more.

I ought to have been a builder. But my father, who built most of the new houses in Mousehole and nearby in the early years of the century, would never let me. "Too hard work, my son," he said. It was, too, in those granite days.

In the little cove called Tavis Vor there was a rock a little way offshore which we called "The Diver". It was our target for a short swim. A little further out, at low tide, was a starting point for a longer swim to Sandy Cove, a matter of a hundred yards or so, following the shore. Sandy Cove at low tide was a good bathing-place, and a good place for learning to swim, if a trifle difficult to get to, over the rocks, for a stranger.

But the magic, of which I spoke a short while ago? I have not forgotten. Yes, the magic of the rocks was still there as I was drawn, mysteriously, to that far cove, a quarter of a mile further on, under Penlee, which had always been known to us as "The Maidens' Cove". We seldom went there. A few girls bathed there, rarely. It seemed somehow to hold us off, to keep its secret. That little cove is beautiful, full of the shore's enamelled mystery, quiet, secluded.

There are massive rocks there, bordering the pebbly sand, separate great stones, the purest specimens of the blue elvan along that stretch of coast. They seem to have been placed there by a giant hand, and, curiously enough, they have little trace of marine growth upon them which makes the elvan look like granite if viewed from a little distance. They are smooth, rounded by the wash of the sea, a lovely elvan blue, and when the tide comes in, partially covering them, and has just receded, leaving them wet, they are bluer still.

It is naturally beautiful, this little cove. The swish and swish of the incoming tide is all that can be heard — a soft music, satisfying to the soul. Kingfishers dart at times among the rocks and pools a little further on.

On my return journey towards the village I wondered what had hapened to the Round Pool and other pools in which many of us had learnt to swim. I found that the Round Pool and others had changed their configuration over the years, owing perhaps to the savage onslaught of eastern gales which had become more frequent over the last twenty or thirty years. There was a small pool, just above the Round Pool, which sloped a little, and was slippery, very smooth on the bottom. We had a name for it which some older people of the village will recall, a quite suitable name, but I will not reveal it here. It was at times in the Summer almost lukewarm. So far, as I write, we have just had a day or two of real Summer warmth. I put my hands in this little pool to test the temperature of the water. It was quite warm.

I sat again on the rocks below "Tavis Vor", looking down towards the Bell Rock and Point Set. One or two small flags were flapping just offshore, in the breeze. They were markers for crab-pots. A picture came into my mind — the famous painting by Millais of the young Raleigh, sitting with a sailor companion, and listening, rapt, to stories of the sea. It made me think of another picture, of a fisherman sitting where I was sitting, looking out into the bay and fashioning at the same time small craft for the children in his charge. I had seen it so often, that picture. The Mousehole fishermen were remarkably fond of children, and painstaking in entertaining them. He used a pocket-knife — a "barber", perhaps, from Howth or Kinsale — for the task, and made two types of craft. One would be constructed from a piece of cork, either picked up on the beach, or brought from some net-loft in the village. The boat would be roughly shaped from the cork. The sails would be thin, shaped parings from a length of wood; they would be inserted into the deck. For keel a thin piece of slate — easily found on the beach — would suffice. The finished product would be called a "carker".

Another boat would be constructed from the stem of a seaside plant of which I forget the name. It was probably of the umbelliferous type, Kex, perhaps. It grew profusely at the base of the cliffs. The sails would be, sometimes, just ivy leaves, but usually sails and keel would be the same as for the "carkers". This boat was, of necessity, of much rougher make-up. It was called a "kisky", which was probably the local, perhaps Old Cornish, name of the plant from which it had been formed.

So the "carkies" and the "kiskies" would be taken down to the children where they sat beside a fair-sized pool, wonder-eyed. They were potential fishermen. They would take great pleasure, with the fisherman's guidance, in sailing the little boats — real luggers, perhaps, in their imagination — across the pool. That particular pool has now, I think, been covered over with concrete, to help for an easier approach to the modern tidal bathing-pool. The pool where the children were testing their primitive craft was always known as "Uncle John Tregenza's Pool" — that was my grandfather. I have never discovered why his name was connected with that pool. Perhaps he had learnt to swim there. I am wrong there, though, for I recollect that my grandfather could not swim at all. I know that he was very fond of fishing, and that, as an old man, he almost failed to scull his punt back into harbour when, after fishing "'tween isle and shore" for pollack, she lost her plug and filled rapidly with water.

XXIII
The Salvation Army

I have spoken of the Methodist Chapels in Mousehole, and it would be unkind if I neglected to tell of the Salvation Army, which played a vital part in the life of the village.

As youngsters we were apt, perhaps, to view it with some wonder, and a little amusement. We were, of course, ignorant of its origins, ignorant that it had been formed as a break-away group from the Methodist New Connection by the Rev. William Booth, in 1865. He and his followers were desirous of less rigid and conventional methods for reaching the poor and neglected in the great cities; for a simpler and more direct presentation of the Christian message. They accepted, like the Protestant churches, the essential Christian beliefs — the immortality of the soul, the resurrection of the body, the eternal happiness of the righteous, and, sad to record, the everlasting punishment of the wicked. Their message was essentially evangelical. They went out among the people, into the streets, into the market-place. They preached repentance, instant salvation, an entire change of life, conversion.

It was not so very different from what one heard in the prayer-meetings and revival services of the Methodist Church.

William Booth evolved gradually a religious organisation with almost military rules and characteristics. He became "General Booth", to be succeeded later by his son, General Bramwell Booth. The rules of the Army were rigidly adhered to, especially by those aspiring to become Officers in the organisation. Candidates for election — women on an equality with men always — were required to observe some quite severe conditions. They could not smoke, or drink, or even take snuff. Some of the conditions, with which I have only lately become acquainted, were certainly hard if obeyed to the letter. Men candidates, for instance, were required not to marry before the age of 23, or, in any case, before they had completed four years in the Service. They were expected to inform their superior Officers, or their Headquarters, if they wished to marry, and to await permission. They could not enter into an engagement unless their superiors were satisfied that the young lady they wished to marry would be likely to make a suitable wife.

Those were some of the conditions, the latter one I have mentioned strange indeed, and hard, surely, to accept. It is to be hoped that they were not always obeyed rigidly, to the letter, and that as time went on it became easier to rise to a position of Officer in the Army.

Looking back, over the years, my impression of that little religious group under the village clock is that they were adhering to a clear and simple faith. It was reflected in what they did, in their immense regard for the unfortunate and poor. It was attractive, that little circle, that band — it was a good band — those women and young girls in their quaint bonnets, so obviously sincere. Their tambourines jingled joyfully to the singing and the music. And, something peculiar to the Salvation Army, I think, there was a sort of happiness there, a note of cheer. They clung to something. They had to, perhaps. And in that they were not alone. Many more highly-gifted intellectually than they in that little circle have found, in the face of life's mystery, the same need to hold on to some pillar of support in the often disturbing contemplation of the vast universe. The great French thinker Pascal, even, felt that same need as he looked up into the heavens that had vouchsafed him no satisfying answer to his immeasurable problems. "Le silence éternal de ces espaces infinis m'effraye!" he declared in his famous work, "Les Pensées". He sought refuge and consolation finally in the Catholic faith.

I like the Salvation Army the more I think about them. I like their simple faith, their untiring social work, their magnificent contribution in times of war. I do not believe that the harsh disciplines to which they had been introduced, and to which they subscribed to the best of their ability, played too great a part in their thoughts. They were concerned with doing good.

One of them would occasionally step out from the circle to give a personal testimony, a story of wrestling with the Devil, of final redemption. I remember Sam Monk stepping out one day, bravely singing, alone.

Many of the old Sankey hymns were sung at their gatherings. We were well acquainted with them in those days. One I remember well: "Bringing in the sheaves". Perhaps the harvest reaped by that little group under the clock was richer than one could have imagined possible.

Their meetings were held usually on Saturday evenings and on Sundays. They would proceed afterwards through the village, gaily, with their band, lingering at various places, such as the Millpool, the Wharf, the Gurnick, always expected and pleasurably received. And grateful for the small contributions placed in their tambourines.

For they were poor. The Officers occupied rooms, when I was a boy, above my father's fish-cellar, at the bottom of Commercial Road. Steps led up — they are still there — to the Captain's modest little apartments, and to what was termed their "Barracks". My grandfather built that fish-cellar, and those Barracks above, in the year 1890. It pleases me that the rent charged by him was very small indeed. My father continued to receive it, quarterly, when my grandfather died. The "Captain" would come down our garden at "Tavis Vor", attractive in her quaint bonnet, with the money. It was just "a few half-crowns", as my brother relates in his book, reminding him, as they dropped upon our table, of the "tinkling tambourines".

The Salvation Army has long gone from the village. The Captain left her little lodging and went down the granite steps for the last time in 1935, by which time the number attending her services had seriously diminished. I don't know where she went — perhaps to the Penzance branch of the Army at their Citadel in Queen Street. But I can imagine that, with her colleagues, she was quite sad in leaving a place she loved, people she loved, and to whom she had given loyal and unselfish service.

I have my own personal remembrance of those standing in that Salvation circle. I know their names. Many of them were poor, had been visited and helped, materially and spiritually, in their homes. They had not forgotten. They kept their allegiance.

At Christmas, at night, often late, the choirs of the Methodists and the Salvation Army would gather together and sing their carols in the gardens and under the windows of the sleeping village.

It was rather wonderful to be awakened then by footsteps and whisperings below, to hear the sudden burst of song in the midnight air. It was Christmas, that strange, religious, magical time, especially for children, when there would be consideration in the minds of men and women, regrets perhaps, resolutions, hope. It is still the same, when Christmas comes and the story of Jesus told.

> We feel regret at Christmas,
> And on Christmas Day,
> For the harsh words spoken,
> And the things we did not say.
>
> And why we groped in darkness
> We cannot truly tell
> Now, at the glad awakening
> Of the Christmas bell.
>
> There's new light up the avenue,
> And new light up the lane,
> And in the radiant morning
> We walk refreshed again.

"While shepherds watched their flocks by night" was perhaps the favourite carol, especially when sung to either of the two familiar Cornish tunes. I have not heard those tunes sung outside the county, but they are impressive, and the Cornish know how to sing them. They hold unaccustomed listeners in awe.

The Salvation Army singers had their own tune, and a conclusion, a sort of chorus, to that wonderful carol, which illustrates well the cheer, the joyousness which was always present in their services:

"Sweet chiming Christmas bells,
Sweet chiming Christmas bells,
They cheer us on our heavenly way
Sweet chiming Christmas bells."

The members of the Salvation Army obeyed strict rules. But they were not aloof. They proclaimed their Evangel in unexpected places. They visited sick rooms and hospitals. They sang willingly upon request in halls of doubtful repute, thereby causing many, perhaps, to reflect, to accept the "gospel", to be "saved". They entered public houses, secure because of their reputation, their obvious sincerity, their happy demeanour. They were quite safe as they distributed their little publications.

Often, in the King's Arms at Paul, on Thursdays, towards evening, I had been expectant to see a young lady Officer of the Salvation Army enter. That was "Susie", as they called her, with her "Young Soldier" and her "War Cry". For them she charged sixpence, but, I am sure, received a good deal more than that from customers of the Inn, who did not necessarily subscribe to her religious views.

She visits still almost every pub in the West Penwith area in the course of a week, driven to them by her own brother.

I have myself asked her to sing. She has a sweet voice. She stands up willingly, and to the strains of "The Old Rugged Cross" or "Amazing Grace" she adds her own personal appeal. She is listened to in silent admiration.

Susie is from the "Citadel", at Penzance. She has been awarded a Certificate held only by a few Salvationists throughout the world, for service which is recognised as outstanding. For many years she has been the official Salvation Army hospital visitor. And many aged people in homes and living alone have reason to be thankful for her cheering presence.

The Certificate was presented to her by the Divisional Commander during a thanksgiving service at the Plymouth Congress Hall.

XXIV
Rescues at Sea, and Tragedy

I stood on the bank at Mousehole as a boy of eleven years old, in November, 1907. It was a dark night, and half a gale blowing. All of a sudden I saw flares go up from the back of the Island, where the sailing barge "Baltic", loaded with cement for some harbour extension work at Newlyn, had run ashore.

The baulks were down in the gaps, and the long-boat that went to her assistance, the "Lady White", skippered by her owner, Stanley Drew, had to be hoisted over them by the crane on the pier-head and deposited in the shallow troughs outside.

The rough journey to the island in that small craft was accomplished successfully by the oarsmen in the "Lady White", and they landed to find that the crew of the barge had managed to get ashore on the island. Indeed, so close had they been that their bowsprit assisted them in their efforts. The survivors were landed with difficulty on to the Old Pier, on the sea side of the baulks, where there was a chain ladder at that time.

This wreck was interesting in the fact that the mate of the "Baltic", Adam Torrie, remained in the village and married Janie Blewett, the harbour-master's daughter, who lived opposite to us in the Millpool. She was sister to Frank Blewett, the longest-serving coxswain of the Penlee lifeboat. I think Adam went back to Ireland for a time, but eventually returned, and his sons are in the village, or near by, still.

Here are the names of the volunteers who manned the "Lady White" on that dark night. Their trip was, needless to say, fraught with danger, especially as they approached the island:

        Stanley Drew (helmsman)
        Willie Harry
        Harry Harvey
        Luther Harvey
        Richard Harry
        Dick Thomas

Stanley Drew was skipper of the pilchard-driver "Ellen", P.Z. 306, the fastest small lugger in the bay. His son, Johnny Drew, was later mechanic on the Penlee lifeboat for 32 years, from 1938 onwards, and still lives in the village.

Richard Harry was father of my cousin Dick Harry. He was a tall, quiet fisherman, who went to sea wearing his bowler hat, like so many of the fishermen in those days.

Dick Thomas was a powerful oarsman, and must have proved a valuable member of that crew. He was a mason who worked with my father in the building trade. His son, Dick Thomas, a mason also, died a short while ago.

The Sailing Barge, "Baltic", ashore on the Island

The crew of the "Lady White"

I have related the story of the "Baltic" because I was so young at the time, and because it has remained vivid in my remembrance.

I saw the early lifeboats, the "Elizabeth and Blanche" and "The Brothers" (the latter the first engine-driven boat) go out many times in terrible weather; upon one occasion when there seemed to be only three or four immense troughs between isle and shore, and we expected to see the lifeboat overwhelmed at any moment.

Apart from the "Baltic", the only other rescue I actually witnessed was in April, 1911, when the S.S. "Cragoswold", of Newcastle, struck the reefs close to the Low Lee Buoy. I was watching at that time from my uncle's house at "Tregonissy". She had come into the bay in rough weather for shelter, having shifted her cargo, and with a dangerous list to starboard. She finally rolled over and sank, only just before the crew of the "Elizabeth and Blanche", then stationed at Newlyn, had taken off the last of her 27 crew.

One of the fishermen watching with us, visibly moved, as indeed we all were, cried out, "She's gone, she's gone! We shaint see she no more!" And that "She's gone, she's gone!" was a label we attached, as rather cruel boys will, to that fisherman for ever afterwards.

The dangers that have to be faced by our lifeboat crews are immense. And never were they more to be feared than upon the night of December 19th, 1981, when in the village we heard the rocket signals for the lifeboat with dismay. For the winds were unusually fierce, and it seemed that no boat could live in the mountainous seas. But the men were called. They went, as they always did, as they always would. They went to a coaster in trouble under Tater Dhu lighthouse, and in the monstrous seas close to the shore, at a given moment, they were overwhelmed, lifeboat and coaster and all, in the terrible shore breakers.

Having rescued a few, miraculously, Trevelyan, the coxswain, decided to go in alongside the coaster again. In that decision by him and his crew, they reached a grandeur to be wondered at, not only by their close relations, but by all feeling men and women of the land. Even grief was somewhat assuaged by the thought of their indomitable courage.

XXV
Memorials

In the Wesleyan Chapel at Mousehole there is a memorial to those brave young men. It consists, first of all, of an octagonal table with an anchor device for centre and the Cap Badge of the R.N.L.I. Along the vertical sides of the octagon are the christian names of the eight members of the crew of the **"Solomon Browne"**. They are written clockwise on the table:

> Trevelyan
> Nigel
> John
> Kevin
> Charles
> Gary
> Barry
> Stephen

    This table was skilfully constructed by Mr. Tom Waters, of Mousehole, from some pitchpine pews in the corner of the Chapel opposite to the memorial.

    There is a brass bell, the gift of the coxswain's mother, Mary, bearing the inscription:

> In loving memory
> of
> William Trevelyan Richards
> Coxswain of the R.N.L.B.
> **Solomon Browne**
> From his mother and family.

    A plaque and Mount were given anonymously, together with the following prayer:

> O God
> Give us serenity to accept
> What cannot be changed,
> Courage to change
> What should be changed,
> And wisdom to distinguish
> The one from the other.
>   Amen.

There is a piano forming part of the memorial, given:

> In loving memory of James Stephen Madron,
> who lost his life in the R.N.L.B. **"Solomon Browne"**,
> 19th December, 1981.
> From his wife Janet, and children Caron and Ian.

There is also a framed little poem by Tom Bellion, entitled **"Solomon Browne"**.

On a seat underneath the separate articles of the memorial there is written:

> "This Chapel of Remembrance was dedicated on Rogation Sunday, 16th May, 1982, to the memory of eight gallant crew members of the R.N.L.B., **"Solomon Browne"**, who lost their lives in the dramatic attempt to save the crew of the "Union Star" on Saturday, 19th December, 1981."
>
> "For greater love hath no man than this: that a man lay down his life for his friends."

I must not forget the striking large representation of the **"Solomon Browne"**, in beaten copper, upon the wall beside the other articles of the memorial, with the words: "Penlee Lifeboat" written aft upon her starboard side.

Alongside the Penlee Lifeboat Slip from which the **"Solomon Browne"** was launched on her last tragic voyage there is to be constructed a Memorial Garden, and in that Garden we shall see a Plaque, donated by the Port Talbot branch of the R.N.L.I. This plaque, of very fine Welsh steel — later to be backed by a heavy block of Welsh slate — bears the following inscription:

To the Proud Memory of

Coxswain	W.T. Richards
2nd Coxswain & Mechanic	J.S. Madron
2nd Mechanic	Nigel Brockman
Emergency Mechanic	John Robert Blewett
Crew Member	Charles Thomas Greenhaugh
Crew Member	Barrie Roberts Torrie
Crew Member	Kevin Smith
Crew Member	Gary Lee Wallis

An impressive coloured picture of the "Solomon Browne" is seen on the top right-hand side of the Plaque.

A map in green shows the general lay-out of the coast where the tragedy occurred — the Inner Buck rock, the position of the wreck of the "Union Star", and various spots where wreckage was subsequently found.

In the bottom right-hand corner of the Plaque is the coloured flag of the R.N.L.I.

This Plaque was formally presented at Mount Zion Methodist Church, Mousehole, by David Aubrey, Honorary Secretary of the Port Talbot Branch, and received by Mrs. Mary Richards, mother of Coxswain Trevelyan.

The following "Description of a Lifeboat", by Sir Winston Churchill, is an interesting feature of this Memorial Plaque:

"It drives on with mercy which does not quail in the presence of death. It drives on as proof, a symbol, a testimony that man is created in the image of God, and that valour and virtue have not perished in the British race."

At the bottom of the Memorial Plaque are words in Welsh:

"CYFEILLION AM BYTH"

of which the English translation is, as far as I have been able to gather:

"Companionship for Life".

Go into the church at Paul. Go down the north aisle — the Newlyn Aisle, as it is sometimes called — towards the impressive granite pulpit built in memory of Robert Wesley Aitken, vicar at Paul for 35 years, who died in 1911. You will find yourself in a space at the back of the choir stalls, just underneath the old limestone pillars and capitals that stand as survivors of the destruction wrought by fire during the Spanish Raid of 1595. If you look up to the wall on your left you will see a suit of armour and two swords supposedly worn long ago by William Godolphin, of Trewarveneth, Squire of the Parish, who died in 1689.

In that quiet spot there is now a striking Memorial to the gallant crew of the ill-fated lifeboat. It was the apt wish of the Church Architect, Mr. John Phillips, R.I.B.A., that the memorial should, in a rugged way, resemble a lighthouse. To achieve that end a huge granite boulder weighing a ton was brought from the foreshore of Lamorna Cove, not far from Tater Dhu and the scene of the disaster — a boulder washed and rounded by the tides, telling the story of the sea and its age-long batterings. That boulder was to represent the tower of the lighthouse.

It was a difficult and laborious task to load the enormous rock, but it was achieved successfully by Mr. George Osborne and his sons. They brought it to Paul Moor, and it was later taken to Porthleven, to the works of a stone-mason, Mr. J.H. Ching, of the firm J. Ching & Sons. There, with the help of Mrs. Kitty Prowse and her assistant, Michael, the stone was chiselled level on the bottom to achieve stability, and on the top also, upon which was to be placed a lantern. A square indentation on the vertical face of the boulder was made to accommodate a Plaque, upon which, later, was the following inscription:

> To commemorate the loss of the crew
> of the Penlee Lifeboat, "Solomon Browne",
> Attempting to save the crew of the "Union
> Star", off Boscawen Cliffs,
> 19 December, 1981.

Written below are the names of the eight members of the lifeboat crew.

The boulder was brought back to Paul, and with the help again of Mr. George Osborne and his sons, placed in the church.

The glazed octagonal Lantern, beautifully constructed, was the work of youngsters dedicated to the task at the Trevenson Industrial Centre, Pool, near Redruth. The youngsters were unemployed, training at the workshop of the Manpower Services Commission. Their Works Manager, Mr. Derek Dixon, came later to the Dedication Service, accompanied by 18-year-old Andrew Bennie, who had helped in the making of the Lantern.

Upon hearing of the tragedy, Mr. B. Jabez Francis, of Peterborough, was moved to send as a gift a beautiful glass crystal Chalice and Paten, in the hope that it might be accepted. It was indeed accepted, gratefully, and placed inside the lantern.

Around the base of the Chalice are the initials of the crew of the lifeboat, and they are also inscribed around the rim of the Paten.

It was sad that Mr. Francis died in the October previous to the Dedication of the Memorial by the Bishop of Truro at Paul Church on Sunday, April 24th, 1983. He was greatly missed at the ceremony, which was attended by the nearest relatives of the lifeboat crew.

The preparation work, the laying of selected slabs of slate for the base of the Memorial, was efficiently carried out by Mr. Alan Jones, builder, assisted by carpenter John Maddern.

Down on the slope to the North Pier at Mousehole there are three strong, comfortable seats, given by the Harbour Authority in memory of the gallant young men of the Penlee Lifeboat.

I sit upon one of those seats on a sunny day and look across the harbour. It is empty,.except for a few small pleasure-boats. The luggers are gone, long gone. But I see them there. I dream of them still, the proud beautiful boats, and of the fine race of men who took them out, in all weathers, often for little gain. They faced great hardship, but they were religiously content, courageous, of the stuff of which lifeboat crews are made.

The tide is full, and I have come to the end of my story. If I give some pleasure to my readers I shall have achieved something worth while. I shall be glad.

* * *

Toll for the Brave

The dark enveloped them
As they rode out
And left the shore,
But in that night
Their light
Was seen no more.

The summons they obeyed,
Sudden, unafraid,
Would be for them a final call,
Would lead them, death defied,
Into the hideous cauldron
Where they died,
Those young men, all.

And there,
Great deeds were done.

Toll for the brave —
They had one life to give,
One precious life,
And that they gave.

* * *